Robby,

Loved meet
Would love to hear
your whole story.
Blessings to you as
you continue on your
journey loving Him!!

Nancy

WHAT GOD?::

Joh 10:10

finding your faith
by Nancy S. Fitzgerald

M000217980

No part of this book may be reproduced for any reason—including reproduction for a retrieval system, or transmission in any form or by any means—electronic, mechanical, photocopy, recording, etc.—without written permission from the author. Reproduction of these materials for any group, school or school system is strictly prohibited.

Copyright © 2008 by Nancy S. Fitzgerald

Published in 2008 by Anchors Away, Inc., Carmel, Ind.

Unless otherwise noted, Scripture quotations have been taken from The Holy Bible: New International Version (NIV). Copyright © 1973, 1978, 1984 by the International Bible Society. Used by permission of Zondervan Publishing House. All rights reserved.

Photography and cover design by Troy Murphy, Launch137, Green Bay, Wis.

All rights reserved. Printed in the U.S.A.

ISBN 978-0-9771828-4-8

This past weekend our extended family gathered at a funeral service to say goodbye to Aunt Jackie. I am always drawn into deeper thoughts about God, life and this world when I attend funerals, no matter who the service is for. Funerals are sobering. As I reflected about Aunt Jackie, I celebrated that she had a full life, yet I would have thought she had much more to live.

I am struck with the reality of how much I don't know. How much more life do I have to live? Who might not be with us the next time we gather as a family?

Connecting with family and friends leads me to a very basic, yet critical question of my life, "what happens after death?" I believe in God and the life He promises, but what do I really know? I find myself searching the deepest parts of my heart to find where my knowledge has become conviction—this thing we call faith. Death will always bring us "face to face" with the validity of our faith and what we believe about God.

What do you believe about God? A deeper question that must come before your answer is, what do you know about Him?

You cannot believe in a God you do not know. How do you know Him? Is it through your parents, friends or religious traditions that you have just accepted? Before you can live your life for God, you must have a faith. A faith comes from a pursuit to come to know this amazing creator.

The pages in this book reveal only a small part of who God is, but they are a great place to start—a way to move forward in understanding more about God, this world and your part in it.

I know that Nancy's great desire is for you to begin the journey to knowing God so that you can live your life for Him, no matter where He takes you. I pray that your heart and mind will be opened to see Him more clearly.

Troy A. Murphy
Pastor, speaker, author, father of four

:: **What God?**

dedication

I am dedicating this book to my children, Scott, Mark, Andrew and Kelly. Thank you for contributing to this book in ways that go way beyond your entries. You are my joy and the reason why I do what I do. I love you.

Mom

:: **What God?**

acknowledgments

Thank you to my former Anchorsaway students who have shared their stories in this book, with the purpose of giving hope and encouragement to those who are trying to figure out what a life with Jesus in the center looks like. Thank you also for your efforts, your passion, your honesty and your willingness to allow us to look into your hearts and into your lives.

Thank you to Agusta Harting, Jim Williams and Jeff Adler, who have given your time and passion to not only teach in your area of expertise, but to minister through the years to hundreds of students in the Anchorsaway classes. Your contributions to this book are invaluable.

Thank you to Julie Spidle with whom I have the pleasure of working on a daily basis and have spent countless hours reading and re-reading and editing this book. Your vision for seeing this book and the Anchorsaway curriculum reach any and every person who is seeking to know their God has been a huge support to me, and life changing for others.

Thank you to my husband, Ed, who thought that retirement from his medical practice meant playing golf, traveling and visiting our kids. For your willingness to edit all of our material many times over, running errands and helping us in any way that we have asked, I am grateful. Your love, support and encouragement go unmatched.

Thank you to all who are striving to live out the Christian worldview with influence, compassion and perseverance. In the midst of this broken world, you haven't given up living out your passion and, as a result, impacting our culture for Christ.

:: **What God?**

:: contents

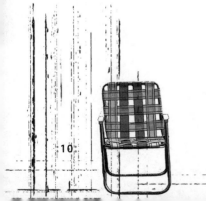

THE LAKE ::

introduction

:: **What God?**

the moment the school bell rang signifying the end of the school year, I, along with my two brothers and sister, were in our car and on the way to our island home at "the lake." Otherwise known as Gull Lake in southwestern Michigan, it is beautiful, crystal-clear and spring fed with sandy shores and sunny skies. There are now 23 homes on the island; some being built back in the early 1900s while others are fairly new. It is not so much a piece of land with houses, but rather a place where families and friends get together during the summer and enjoy all that the lake has to offer.

Some call it serendipitous, and for good reason. Where else can you go where there are no cars, and the only traffic are the residents of the island and their dogs walking around the shoreline while the kids try out the various rope swings hanging from the branches of several big oak and maple trees that line the water's edge? As young children, we spent our days playing croquet, building paths into the woods in the middle of the island and building and rebuilding club houses out of pieces of scrap wood and fallen branches. We swam in the water, fished, netted turtles and skied whenever possible. To this day, little has changed. Life at the lake was good, very good. One day would flow into the next and soon it was time to move back into town and prepare to go to school once again.

There was, however, one day I will never forget. I was 5 years old and my older sister, Carole, was 7. We were in our yard engaged in a game of croquet while our two-year-old brother, Stephen, was in the house with our babysitter. My mother had gone into town, as she did every week, to do the laundry. My father was at work and my older brother, Joel, was at camp. Our playing was interrupted by a shout from our babysitter, "Where is Stephen?"

"We don't know," we replied.

"Carole, you go into the woods and look for him. Nancy, you look for him on the dock. I'll check in the house once again."

I went running out on the dock shouting his name, "Stephen, where are you?

Ste-e-e-ephen!" It was nothing new for Stephen to run off. He had done this several times before, and I kept thinking that any moment he would pop his blond, curly head around the corner of the boathouse, flashing his big, toothy grin. I looked all over the boathouse and in the boats, but there was no Stephen to be found. Assured that he was not out there, I began to walk down the dock and back in toward the house. Something caught my eye by the shoreline. It was Stephen. He was face down and floating in the water. I shouted to the babysitter and then jumped in trying desperately to rescue him. I tried to pick him up to lift him out, but being small myself, I could not budge him.

Within seconds, the babysitter leapt into the water herself and picked Stephen up in her arms. Water was streaming off his face and down his hair. His once active little body was still. "What's wrong with Stephen?" I asked.

"He's dead, and it's your fault," she screamed. With that, she ran with Stephen in her arms, out of the water and to the neighbor's house. Carole and I were left alone to ponder what had just happened. It was the last time we saw Stephen.

Soon the yard was filled with crowds of friends and strangers. Some were crying loudly, while others stood and hugged each other. My mother was surrounded with friends and my father sat in a chair with his head buried in his hands. I stood numb, empty and scared; there was no lap to sit in or arms to fall into. Alone, I retreated into the house and into my parents' bedroom.

Like so many families, we went to church on Sundays. We said grace before our dinner meal. At night, before bed, we would always pray, "Now I lay me down to sleep. Pray the Lord my soul to keep and if I die before I wake, I pray the Lord my soul to take. Amen." I knew that Jesus loved me, because the Bible told me so, at least that's what the song said. I believed that God was good and could do anything. With that kind of child-like faith, I pleaded with God.

"God, I know you can make Stephen better. Please don't let him die." There was nothing else to say. I knew God could help people and Stephen was just a baby, so of course He would help him. Why not? Isn't that what God does? Help people?

With that I went to be with my sister and, after what seemed like eternity, my father came to my sister and me and informed us that Stephen had died and now he was in heaven.

Alone and afraid, I retreated back into my parents' bedroom, and once again addressed God. "Why didn't you make Stephen live? Are you going to kill me, too? Maybe you're not as good as people say you are. You scare me. Who are you REALLY, God?" At that moment, I walked out of the bedroom and away from God for the next 27 years.

A part of me died that day, as I think it did with many of us. For me, it was the end of the innocence of youth. Nothing was certain any longer, not even God. I felt alone and scared of life and of death. I would never be the same.

Life went on, as it does when tragedy happens, but my encounter with death and the guilt attached to it lingered for years to come. In those days people weren't very good about processing traumatic events, so very little was ever mentioned from that day on about Stephen, or how we children were dealing with such a horrific catastrophe. Joel, Carole and I did not attend the funeral for whatever reason. We spent the rest of the week with our grandparents and then we went back to the lake and were expected to live as if nothing had happened. There was, however, a constant reminder of that dreadful day at the lake: Stephen's empty crib remained in my bedroom for the rest of that summer. The emptiness of the crib did not compare to the barrenness of my soul.

Several years later, I was sitting in my eighth grade science class. This particular day we were talking about the properties of water, and I remember my teacher explaining to our class that although water was made up of hydrogen and oxygen, you still couldn't breathe while under the water. The next thing I remember was getting extremely lightheaded, and then I passed out. I was taken to the hospital and given a multitude of tests, but no one could figure out what was wrong with me.

The next day, a friend of my parents, who was a child psychologist, came to visit me in the hospital. We chatted for a little while and then he asked me a question: "Do you ever think about Stephen?"

I was shocked at the question, because we never felt comfortable talking about him. "Yes, I do," I responded and then said very matter-of-factly, "You know, I killed him."

I will never forget the look on Dr. C's face. "You what?" he responded. "Nancy, look at me. You did not kill him. You were five years old, for God's sake. You were not the babysitter. You did not kill him! Hear me, you did not kill him!" More than his words of exoneration was the look of horror on his face that told me once and for all that it was not my fault that Stephen died. It was an amazing and freeing revelation for me, but the greater issue remained: "Who are you really, God? Can I trust you? Are you good or evil?"

As the excitement of being in high school approached, the weightiness of my questions about God was pushed to the outer recesses of my mind. I didn't think too much about God during those years; the pain of losing Stephen was dulled by the busyness of life, which for me was all about fitting in and having fun. By the time I was a senior in high school, my focus had turned to my future. "Where should I go to college? What should I study? What's it going to be like when I get there? Can I do the work?"

I ended up attending and graduating from Indiana University with three degrees in education and the sciences. I loved every minute of it, and would not have traded those experiences or friendships for anything in the world.

Toward the end of my college experience, I would often wonder, "What is my purpose in life? Is there a God?" I would engage in conversations with all kinds of people with different backgrounds and different beliefs about their purpose in life. From Christians to atheists, most of them said that their purpose in life was to make a lot of money, get a good job and enjoy life.

Through those times of questioning others, it was the group called "Christians" that I found to be most interesting. They all would acknowledge that they believed in God, but when I pressed them for the reason why they believed in God, not one of them could give me a reason that made sense. The answers were unbelievably shallow and sadly, pretty much the same: "I grew up that way." "It makes me feel good." "My parents told me so." I would ask over and over again for them to give me the reason why they believed and the difference God had made in their lives. Not one single person could give me a reason for the hope that they had in Jesus Christ that made sense to me as someone who was searching for truth. Not a single one! I was frustrated and disgusted that intelligent people would identify with Christianity but had absolutely no idea if what they believed was true. My soul knew I needed God but my mind was totally turned off.

I became very cynical toward Christianity and Christians in general. My natural inclination was to conclude that this whole Christian thing was either a hoax or an extremely restrictive way of living for the weak-minded. I soon came to the conclusion that my purpose in life was to have fun and take from life as much as I possibly could. The last person in the world that I desired to be was a Christian.

Have fun I did. I went to Florida during my junior year for spring break and met a guy named Ed who was cute and rode on an Indiana University bike team. (My own children could never understand why they were not allowed to go to Florida for their spring breaks.) His team had come to Florida to practice for the Little 500 bike race and, like the rest of us, to have a whole lot of fun meeting people, relaxing on the beach and partying. Despite being on the same campus, we had never met. We had a wonderful time getting to know each other and continued our new found relationship when we returned to school.

He loved athletics, was adventurous and just plain nice. To my surprise, I found that he was one of the few people I had met during my college experience that thought about something other than the next weekend's party schedule. Ed had a goal of wanting to go to medical school and fulfill his dream of being a thoracic surgeon. He wanted his life to count. We continued to spend lots of time together through the next few years. We got to know each other's families and he and my dad became best friends as they went fishing and bird hunting together. That was a big deal for me because my dad and I were extremely close, and his approval of Ed was very important to me. Probably the best thing that I liked about him was that he loved me just as I was. After I finished graduate school and Ed completed his second year of medical school, we decided that we would get married, some day buy a house, have kids, play golf and live the "good life."

Marriage began just as we had planned: I went to work teaching, and he went to work learning medicine. We were dirt poor, but didn't mind it. In retrospect, it was very good for us, because we were on our own and had to depend on each other. We lived in a tiny apartment and found that we could be happy eating a nice dinner or slightly burnt grilled cheese sandwiches. On Friday nights, if we had enough money left over, we would buy a soda for each of us and watch a movie on TV. We had lots of great memories, but looked forward to the day when we could someday get a home, and go to the grocery store without having to return half the stuff in our cart, because we ran out of money.

When Ed completed medical school, we moved to Hershey, Pennsylvania, where he began his surgical residency at the Hershey Medical Center. Our dream of a perfect life began to take an unhealthy turn as we saw less and less of each other. He was on call almost every night at the hospital, and so I decided that I would play lots of golf tournaments and seriously considered becoming a professional golfer. I traveled all over the country that year, playing in amateur and professional events, but soon decided that it was not the life for me. It was too difficult traveling in a car, staying in motels and being with people with whom I had very little in common outside of golf. I returned home with Ed and told him that I just wanted to be with him and have kids and play golf as an amateur. He was pleased and also wanted to start a family. Our first son, Scott, was born, and then 15 months later, our son, Mark, was born. Being a mom brought more joy to me than I could ever imagine.

The dream of being happy and having this perfect life, however, was developing a few more cracks. Ed was gone so much of the time that when it was time for the kids to go to bed, Scott would run and Mark would crawl to the coat rack, knowing they were in for a ride to the hospital to say "good night" to their dad. We hoped that he would be home to see us the next day or so. Needless to say, we both looked forward to the time when the five-year residency would end and Ed would became a "real" doctor, and wouldn't have to work so hard. That was a long time to endure. I just hoped that we could make it work until then.

Not only did I have concern about my life with a husband who was rarely home and had fallen in love with his work, but I also had this uncontrollable fear that the boys would stop breathing as they slept. I woke up in the middle of every night and checked to see if they were both breathing. When satisfied that they were going to make it through the night, I would go back to bed and try to salvage a little more sleep before the next busy day began. I longed to get the rest that I needed, the peace of mind about death, and the comfort of knowing that my marriage was going to survive. Without God, all I could do was to be taken hostage by these feelings and to live under the veil of doubt and fear.

Finally, the residency was over and it was time to say good bye to beautiful Hershey, and hello to a new life in Indianapolis. Now was the time for our dream lives to begin; we moved into a real home in a great neighborhood filled with kids! This was what we had been waiting for for the last eight years. I was going to raise the kids, play golf, get involved in the community, while Ed was going to join a medical group and do heart and lung surgery. He would be home at five every night and we could begin to live out the American dream … wonderful family and a happy marriage. At least that was my plan.

My life and Ed's life became extremely busy: he, with his practice in Indianapolis, and mine with the job/privilege of raising our children. Within the next year and a half, I had given birth to our third son, Andrew, and then to our daughter, Kelly. I absolutely loved our kids and would do whatever it took to make sure that they were happy and healthy. Yes, I still continued my night vigil of checking to make sure that all four kids were breathing. Ed's practice was going well, perhaps too well. We could go days without seeing him and when we did, he was understandably exhausted.

In spite of all the family and material blessings, in my heart of hearts there was no peace, purpose or joy. I felt empty inside. There was something very wrong. "Was this all there was to life?" I had tried to do everything that was right, and still I had no feeling of fulfillment. Ed had provided for us everything and more than we needed. On the outside, we had lived out the American dream. But to what avail? The one thing I did know was that happiness and peace and joy were not found in the material world: in our jobs, our houses, our children, spouses or friends. Could it possibly be connected in any way to God? Was there a God? Might there be One who could give me a little peace of mind? My search to find God began. In spite of the Christians I knew, I needed to find out for myself if there truly was a God who cared.

What did the different religions have to say about God and about this person called Jesus Christ? After several visits to the local library, I was totally perplexed. I learned about Hinduism by reading through the Bhagavad Gita, which was an interesting read, but it did not answer my question as to who God is. I found that to the Hindu, God was not seen as a personal God, but rather, as an "it." In popular Hinduism there may be many gods. In a very real sense they believe that man can become a "god." That wasn't going to do it for me.

What about Buddhism? I found that they vary from sect to sect. Most Buddhist sects are polytheistic, pantheistic or atheistic, take your pick. Truth is found through enlightenment, which is the living power for good. Truth must be worked out in the mind. They believed that Buddha has found the truth, and only he can proclaim it. That fascinated me because Buddha never claimed to be God. I found nothing tangible for me to hold onto with this religion and so my search continued.

A look into Islam didn't give me much hope either, especially as a woman. A woman is traditionally seen as property, with little, if any, value. Although most of us think of the Koran as being the only holy book of Islam, I was surprised to find that one of their holy books is the Injil, which is the New Testament. Still, Jesus is not seen as their Savior, but only a prophet of God.

I found it interesting that neither Hinduism, Buddhism nor Islam recognized or accepted Jesus Christ as the Messiah. All three religions believed that their salvation came through some form of works. "How much work must I do to know and be accepted by God?" I would ask. No one ever gave me an answer other than …"You just keep working!" I was not going to work myself to death, only to find that it wasn't enough to get to heaven. One thing I knew for sure, all religions were not the same. It was time for me to take a very serious look at Christianity to see what it had to say about Jesus Christ and their holy book, the Bible, despite my bias against Christians.

Not long after my search for truth began, I was invited to go to Florida with some friends of mine. I was thrilled to get away to rest, play golf and to look into the Bible for the first time, to see if it had anything to say about life and this person, Jesus. I remember packing a very skinny Bible, because I figured that it was easier to read than a thick one. I arrived early and anxiously began reading the Bible from page one. Now was my time of seeing what all the Jesus stuff was about. My enthusiasm quickly waned; it didn't take me long to see that this book was as confusing as the other religious ones I had read. I read through Genesis and glanced through Exodus and slogged my way through the beginning of the book Leviticus. Frustrated, I came to the conclusion that there was no Jesus Christ in the Bible and God seemed to be a bit too testy. Frankly, I found it all to be confusing and of little value in giving me the key to purpose, joy and hope in this life and the next, if there was one. I became discouraged as I realized that if there is no God, then there is no hope, and things for me were only going to get worse. "Who and where are you, God?"

Matthew 7:7-8 (Jesus speaking) "Ask and it will be given to you; seek and you will find; knock and the door will be opened to you. For everyone who asks receives; he who seeks finds; and to him who knocks, the door will be opened."

Unaware of who God was, and totally ignorant as to the nature of God, He began to show His love, mercy and faithfulness to me. He had arranged for me to stay with a friend of mine, Cookie, who was one of those "born again Christians." I gathered up my courage and confided in her that I was searching for God or this Jesus, but could find nothing in the Bible that had made any sense to me. She lovingly told me that the Bible was made up of 66 books, and a good place to start was in the middle with the New Testament book of John. With love, encouragement and a lot of patience, she was willing to answer all kinds of questions that I had about life, about God and death. Her text was the Bible. By the end of the third chapter of John, God had begun to answer the questions I had been pondering since the day Stephen died.

That evening, when everyone else had gone to bed, I once again began to pray to God. I simply told Him that I had no clue as to who He really was, that I was lost and in great need of peace and joy. I told Him that if He were truly the God of the Bible, author of life and giver of peace, to please come into my inner being, change my heart and give me peace and joy and love, which I so desperately needed. I informed Him that under no circumstance was I going to go to Africa, nor would I be any kind of the missionary type person, nor would I ever tell anyone what I just did. I was fearful that if He was really God, He might change me into one of those "weird Christians" to whom I had developed a disliking. Giving up control did not sit well with me but I asked Him to show Himself as real to me, and if He would do that, I would give my every remaining day to serve Him.

There are no words to explain what had happened to me, but I can tell you that my interest in playing in that golf tournament was gone; I could not wait to get home to my kids and to my husband. I came back physically and spiritually refreshed. For the first time that I could remember, I was filled with a peace that had no words of explanation. I resumed my role as a mom and a wife, but with new excitement and energy. After a few weeks of being home, it occurred to me that I no longer woke up at night to check on the kids' breathing. Ed began to notice a change. He said he thought I had gone on vacation to play some golf and hang out with the girls, but that I had come back a different person. He told me that I left uptight and anxious, and now there was a peace about me that he had never seen, but desperately needed for himself. At that very moment, I knew that God was faithful to show Himself to me. He was who He said He was; He was God and He was alive in me! I shared with Ed what I had found to be true about God, but that my journey had just begun. I told him that I knew very little about God, but that if he read the book of John, he might begin to figure it out, as well.

Ed found a Bible and also read the book of John, and he also dared to believe that Jesus was who He said He was, God. Our new, but far from perfect, lives had begun. We both knew that we lived in a broken world that was filled with broken people. We were those people. But as imperfect as we were, God was faithful to show Himself to us and give us that peace and joy and life purpose for which we both yearned.

Believing that Jesus Christ died for me and rose again so that I, and others who believe, could have life and have it to the full, signified just the beginning of my search. I had questions that had been on my heart for years: Who is God? How can I know Him for sure? From where did I come and when I die, where am I going? Why is the world in such a mess and in the midst of that, what is my purpose in life? How can I be sure that the Bible stands alone and apart from all other books and is truly God's Word? Can I learn such things? My journey was one where I was looking for answers beyond emotions and opinions of others. I had to find out for myself what was true, and separate that from religion and man's imagination. I was going to study the findings from other writers of antiquity, students of the Scriptures, archaeologists, as well as the best thinkers of our time. Not only did I need to find answers for myself, but for my family, as well. They needed to know the truth about God so that they could live their lives with assurance and with hope, and not the fear and anxiety that I had been carrying around for years. God gave me a voracious appetite for knowing truth and for teaching it to anyone who would listen. Strangely enough, those feelings remain as strong today as they were then.

As our children grew up, I took great joy in praying for them and sharing with them some of what I was learning about this great God we worship. Ed and I tried to live out the Christian worldview on a daily basis as best we could. It was not so much what we did, but the attitude that God gave us to become better listeners, lovers of others and much more compassionate, with still much room for growth. We would also get up early in the morning and have a short Bible study with the kids and spend some time praying together. It became a special thing for our busy family to do, because it was the one time of each day that we were all together. We tried to put God first in our lives. We failed more than we succeeded, but in spite of us, God continued to show His faithfulness and mercy to our family.

When our oldest son, Scott, was preparing for college, I realized that in spite of all that we had done in trying to prepare him for leaving home, he was far from ready. He knew God, loved his family, but he was clearly not ready to contend with the conflicting worldviews that he was about to encounter as he walked onto the college campus of his choice.

That was when God began to birth in me the idea of taking the research that I had completed from the questions I had about God and Christianity and write a curriculum, now called Anchorsaway. It was to be specifically for seniors in high school and college students, preparing them not only to defend what they knew to be true about God and the Bible, but to be lights in a messed up world wherever God would choose to take them. My first class to try out this rather raw curriculum was our son, Scott's, class at church almost 18 years ago.

> **Scott's Story.** The first class of Anchorsaway met at church on Sundays with about six or seven other seniors. I remember learning about the reliability of the Scriptures, and left the study believing more in God and the Bible. We were all given choices as to how we were going to live it out and it was there that I made a bad choice. I was not totally convinced that I wanted to set my mind on God's purpose for my being at college, because I was afraid that I was going to miss out on being a part of the group that was having fun. Once on campus, it didn't take long for me to become derailed. There were way more temptations, coupled with lots of free time, that I was not expecting. I made the mistake that many kids my age make in thinking that somehow it won't happen to me. I made way too many poor decisions that first year by not going to class and drinking. I realized what had happened, and by the grace of God, I was given another chance to prove that I could make good choices and do what it took to graduate well from college. I graduated and am now married, have two daughters and my own business. I thank God to this day that He is who He says He is: a God of second chances!

Yes, that first year of preparing the seniors for their after-high-school experience was a bit rough for all of us. Each year following, I would continue to study, talk with my former students, add to the lessons already written, and write new chapters as I felt they were needed. The focus of the curriculum became one of learning not only why we believe, but how we live our lives and love those who are different in thought and lifestyle. Anchorsaway is published and is being taught in homes across America and in countries around the world!

The remainder of this book is the findings from my personal quest to find what is true about God, the Bible, life and death. This is combined with personal stories from my own life as well as those from several former students and teachers. Their stories deal with their own personal lives, including their doubts and fears about God and life, and how they found peace and purpose and forgiveness. These friends contributed their stories with the hope that it might, in some way, positively impact and encourage you on your life journey. Not all of the stories have happy endings. Real life is like that. :: :: ::

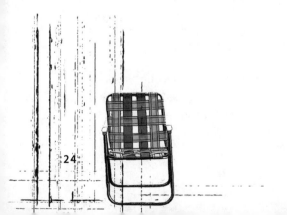

PREACHERS ::

chapter 1

:: **What God?**

i used to think that all people were basically similar and that we all

believed in pretty much the same thing. It didn't take me long to realize that
was simply not true. All people do not believe the same about much of
anything, especially God. Is He personal or distant? Is He loving and forgiving,
or judgmental and demanding? Am I God, or am I to worship a God beyond
myself? Is there such a thing as God? Maybe there are lots of Gods, or just one
God. The questions are unending, as are people's opinions of whom or what
God might be like. One thing is for sure; most people will give a strong,
emotional opinion of what they think about the whole God issue. You don't
have to wear a black robe with a collar to preach about God. In our culture,
some of the most vocal preachers about God (or lack thereof) are professors,
scientists, writers, television news anchors, movies, movie stars, music and
perhaps your best friend. The list is unending.

In the true sense of the word, all of us are preachers. The way we think, interact
with one another, and our opinions about people and things in our lives all set
the foundation for our "sermons." For me, because I didn't believe in the God of
the Scriptures, I lived according to my own set of rules and I decided what was
right and wrong. Life, quite simply, was all about me. Being successful,
accepted and materially comfortable was my goal, and therefore, all I said and
how I lived reflected my own "me-centered" goals in life. If there was a God, I
figured that He graded on the curve and that because I never killed anyone and
volunteered a bunch, I was, if need be, "in." Without saying a word, I was
preaching to everyone I met. No, I wasn't standing on a street corner yelling at
people, but I was preaching my beliefs by the way I lived, my moral convictions
and by how and what I communicated to others. I was simply living out my
worldview.

Worldviews are similar to wearing a pair of glasses. We all wear them. The color
of the lenses we have in our glasses will determine how we see things. If you
have a pair of glasses with blue lenses in them, everything will look blue.
Wearing a pair of glasses with red lenses will cause everything to appear red.
What we believe in our hearts to be true will determine how we live and how

we interact with and see the world around us. We reflect our worldview by the way we speak, dress, spend money, love others, work at our jobs and live out our life in general.

As there are many different colors of lenses from which to choose, so are there a multitude of worldviews. The most prevalent ones in life are: the Christian worldview, the Naturalist worldview, the Postmodernist worldview, the Pantheistic worldview and the Spiritist worldview. No one person lives strictly within a worldview, but their foundational beliefs will generally fall into one of the five mentioned. In my search for knowing God, it became extremely important to me to see if the Christian worldview and other worldviews could answer basic life questions in a way that explains life and gives hope. The basic questions that most all people have about life are: From where did I come? Why is there such a mess in the world? Is there any hope? What is my purpose here on earth? What happens when I die?

It was these questions that motivated me to search for answers. Did the Christian worldview answer these questions in a way that made sense and could be verified? As I continued to grow in my own personal faith in Christ, I discovered that the answers were clear, complete and provable. What about the other worldviews? How do they answer those life questions? Studying the other worldviews was extremely valuable to me, and hopefully to you, because it taught me what worldview I was living out. I also learned how to better understand from where people were coming philosophically, as well as how I might better communicate with those who think and believe differently than I did. The remainder of this chapter is an overview of the five worldviews.

:: An overview of the Christian worldview

The foundation of the Christian worldview is based on the Bible being the Word of God. From the Scriptures we know that Jesus died on a cross for the sins of the world, was buried and on the third day rose again.

John 3:16-18 (Jesus speaking) "For God so loved the world that he gave his one and only Son, that whoever believes in him shall not perish but have eternal life. For God did not send his Son into the world to condemn the world, but to save the world through him. Whoever believes in him is not condemned, but whoever does not believe stands condemned already because he has not believed in the name of God's one and only Son."

Upon belief, God sends the Holy Spirit, the Comforter, to dwell in believers and guide them in living out their faith in every area of life. I am not talking about a Christian being perfect. What I believe Scripture teaches us is that, as believers, we are forgiven from the penalty of sin, but we still sin. God expects us to not only know Him, but also to communicate with Him through prayer. His desire for us is to live out our life so as to positively impact culture for His sake. We are called to be givers, not takers, and men and women with servants' hearts, as we interact with those around us. Needless to say, living out this kind of a life does not come naturally, but is rather the result of us choosing, through a series of good choices, to love God with all our heart, mind and soul.

As a nonbeliever in Jesus Christ for many years, one of the biggest turnoffs for me was, and still is, a self-righteous "born-again Christian" who pretends to know all the answers and lead a perfect life. Many of these people are the ones who only want to be heard and the only language they know how to speak is "Christianese." That is not a picture of one who is truly living out the Christian worldview. The good news is that there are many who are actually living out the Christian worldview. One of my former students, Brett, stands out as someone I will never forget, as one who embraced life, Christ and others with endless zeal.

Brett's Story. Many words could describe the person of Brett Michael Hershey; fun-loving, kind, generous, the life of the party, a great friend, respected fraternity member and well-loved brother. But the one characteristic that stood out to everyone was his love for Jesus Christ. His relationship with God was what defined him, more than anything else.

Brett grew up in a family that honored God, lived out their faith and ministered to others. His parents, Roger and Roxanne, were on staff with Campus Crusade for Christ, and raised their family of four in the midst of Bible studies and fellowship with college students. Never to be one to sit on the sidelines, Brett sat in on outreach events and played football with the big kids. Even as a boy, he loved being with people and making them laugh. His young faith was expressed in earnest prayers to God, trusting Him for big and little things in life.

As a senior, Brett told everyone about a Bible study for seniors that met on Sunday evenings. He was a bit like the Pied Piper. Where Brett went, many followed. He participated in the Anchorsaway nights with great enthusiasm, bringing his believing friends as well as nonbelievers with him. Never in a hurry to leave after the evening's lessons, Brett would always stay to make sure all the cookies were eaten and to have more time hanging out with his friends.

As his senior year in high school came to an end and classmates were deciding on where to go to college, Brett made an unusual decision. Yes, he wanted to attend Indiana University, but first, he enlisted in the National Guard. His reasons were twofold: he wanted to serve his country and he wanted to share Christ with fellow soldiers.

Brett's ministry at college was not limited to one night a week or church on Sunday mornings. He joined Sigma Chi fraternity and was a key player in initiating a new outreach ministry to students in the Greek community. Brett led a Bible study in his fraternity and pursued relationships with both Christian and non-Christian brothers to build into their lives.

For three years he lived college life to the fullest while living out his Christian faith unashamedly. Many would say that the two cannot go together; that you cannot have true fun and follow Christ at the same time. Brett would disagree and so would his friends. For Brett led the example of living a life of freedom. He could have fun and laugh and make others laugh as a result of the joy that spilled over from his close walk with Jesus.

Brett would be the last person in the world to claim perfection. When people thought of Brett, they thought of a normal guy with an awesome faith in the almighty God! Brett's life reflected a man who had an authentic faith in Christ and was not afraid to live out the Christian worldview.

:: An overview of the Naturalist/Humanist worldview

Sadly, not everyone has a faith like Brett's. John, for example, was extremely bright and a born leader. He was also a self-professed atheist. His ambition was to become an engineer and make enough money to live the "good" life. Some of his friends were Christians who would try to reason with him about God. John got sick and tired of being bugged by his friends about his beliefs, and decided that he would make a list of the reasons that he could not believe in God and gave it to them. On his list, John said that there was nothing about life that man couldn't remedy. He believed that man "invented" God because they were not smart enough to figure life out for themselves.

Instead of believing that God created, he believed that man evolved over millions of years. The world is a mess because man hasn't figured out how to make it right. When asked what was going to happen to him when he died, he would laugh and say that he was going to become worm food. John was living out the Naturalist/Humanist worldview. He rejected a belief in God, but gave in to his friend's request to come to an Anchorsaway class to get some answers to some of his beliefs. He came and after several weeks of class and rehashing the material during the week with friends, he finally saw that the Bible was true and, therefore, God had to be who He says He is. John grew in his faith and during his commencement talk as president of his class, gave a beautiful testimony on the love of God.

:: An overview of the Postmodernist worldview

It is no secret that most cultures today are steeped in trappings of the Postmodern worldview. Like John's former belief in Naturalism, the Postmodernist rejects God and His moral laws. Each person is left to decide his own standards by which to live, leaving each person to direct his life through subjective feelings. In the purest form, Postmodernism leads to a life without hope. Simply put, there are no moral absolutes. Do whatever you want to do and believe whatever you want to believe, because there is no universal truth. What you do is good for you and what I do is good for me.

Matt and Andy are twins, and as seniors in high school, they were wonderful basketball players, good students and loved to party. They professed outwardly to be Christians, but in truth they were Postmodernists that came reluctantly to the Anchorsaway class. There they learned that God gives each one of us the right to choose to be obedient and follow Him, or to simply do our own thing and follow the world. Sadly, both Matt and Andy had this notion that God was withholding fun and good times from them, and so they reasoned that to enjoy the good times in college, they had to do it without accountability and without God directing their lives. They had forgotten that there can be heavy consequences for bad life choices.

Matt's Story. I did not grow up in a Christian family. We didn't attend a Bible-believing church. Basketball is what was most important to me and what was ingrained in my soul as most important. My goal in life was to be as successful as possible in the world's eyes and make a ton of money.

One night when I was in sixth grade, I was having a sleepover with my friend Ben. It was raining very hard and I started to get scared. Much to my embarrassment, I started to cry in front of Ben. So to get my mind off of my emotions, I posed a question to Ben. I said, "Did you know that when it is raining outside robbers can break in, because you can't hear them break in?" I even went so far as to tell Ben that they could kill us.

To my surprise, Ben came back with the question, "If you died today would you go to heaven or hell?"

I was floored by that question. My comeback was, "No one can know for sure." But I felt like I had done more good than bad, so I would probably go to heaven.

Ben then told me that he knew of a way to know for sure. This intrigued me. Ben told me that I could accept Christ and receive salvation. Ben and I prayed together and for the first time in my life I began to understand that God was loving, forgiving and personal. Ben went home the next morning, and because my family was not Christian I didn't take this new found interest in God any further. I didn't really have a good understanding of what a real and authentic relationship with God might look like.

A couple of years later, my parents became Christians. My twin brother, Andy, and little brother, Todd, had also become Christians. But by this time my mind had already been set. I thought basketball was really important, as well as having lots of friends and girlfriends. Being popular was on the top of my priority list. To me, that is what it was all about. So by the time my parents tried to get me to go to church, I had hardened my heart and my ears to hearing anything that was said. This caused me to be really cold towards God.

By the time senior year came around, my twin brother and I had received Division 1 scholarships to play basketball. We knew we were going to college for free, so we didn't have to worry about school or how to pay for it. Come to think of it, I didn't have to worry about much of anything my senior year. Therefore, I allowed my life to get out of control very quickly. At the end of the year, my parents strongly recommended that I come to the Fitzgerald's house and participate in Anchorsaway. So I went, really not wanting to go, but once I tasted the chocolate chip cookies, I knew I would come back every week!

Over the weeks of teaching from Nancy, I clearly remember thinking that I was headed off to college in California where nobody knew me. I could completely change my life and be someone other than who I currently was and live for Christ. I didn't have any friends at college, nor did I have anyone I knew that would be tempting me. I really considered which way

I would live my life. Would I continue living the way I was living, headed on a downward spiral, or would I follow Christ? Unfortunately, I made a decision to continue living my life my way and leave God out of the picture.

I went to California and fell deeper and deeper into drugs, alcohol and the sinful life. By the time I came home my first summer, between my freshman and sophomore years, my life was so out of control that I fell into a really deep depression and had a lot of different problems. I left for my sophomore year in college, and while in California, I fell into an even deeper depression, so deep that I was hospitalized for it. My doctor recommended that I come home to Indiana and spend a year here. So I did, and was hospitalized for a few more weeks in Indianapolis. This was a difficult transition for me, because I lost the constant companionship of my twin brother, with whom I was very close. I had also lost basketball, an activity that, for years, was my whole world, and in what I placed my hope for my future …

During that time, my life was spiraling out of control and I was falling deeper and deeper into a sinful life. In January of that year, my best friend, Ben, who had brought me to Christ, had passed away. I incurred a ton of guilt as a result of Ben's death, because Ben was also in rehab, and he had asked me to pick him up and show him a good, clean, fun time. Unfortunately, I could not promise him that. Ben was found dead two days later after checking himself out of rehab. The guilt from Ben's death has been very difficult for me, still to this day. At this time in my life, I had no idea where to go, what to do, or with whom to talk. Finally, on February 11th I went upstairs, packed up my room and car, and wrote a poem asking God to get me out of the concrete I was in. I was sinking fast and needed a way out.

Fortunately, God did do something for me that next morning. He sent an IPD officer at 4 a.m. to arrest me for going the wrong way down a one-way street. I had controlled substances in my car and was drinking and driving, as well. By the graciousness of the judge, I was released from jail and sent immediately to a rehab center in Arizona.

Matt's choices reflect the Postmodern worldview, because he rejected God and made up his own rules for living. He made choices that, at the time, felt good and were accepted by the culture in which he lived, but produced much pain, suffering and despair. This Postmodern way of looking at the world puts all responsibility and blame on each individual and his or her choices.

"The Postmodern heartbeat has pumped cynicism through the veins of our culture; we are distrusting of almost everything. There is no truth, no meaning, no certainty. Yet, even in such a distrusting worldview, trust of the self is the one thing that seems to be left unquestioned. The warning of Dostoevsky no doubt explains the contradiction. When God is dead, someone or something will take his place. Someone will always be Lord. Self, interpretation and taste are currently popular rulers among us, and trusting one's heart has become the religion of choice."[1]

:: An overview of the Pantheistic worldview
What do Star Wars, The Lion King, Pocahontas, Scientology, Dianetics and the New Age have in common? They all reflect the Pantheist worldview. The Pantheist believes that God is a part of the creation, not separate from it. God is in everything and everyone. The universe and everything in it is divine, therefore, everything is interconnected. Truth to the Pantheist comes through "oneness with the universe." The Pantheist agrees with the Humanist and the Postmodernist that the universe created itself. The only hope is to connect more deeply and harmoniously with the universal nature in other humans. Their purpose is to encourage others to join them in this universal effort to create perfect harmony. The Pantheist believes that upon death, the body will die, and then go through many rebirths or reincarnations, until it eventually becomes one with the universe.

This "spiritual" worldview is found, not only in movie theaters and cults, but has worked its way into the church, education, sports and medicine, to name a few. One thing that we know about Satan is that he is an imitator, but not a creator. His pattern for working is easy to spot once you know for what you are looking. For the western Pantheist, the way to live in harmony, oftentimes, is through ancient arts of meditation (not biblical), yoga, behavioral therapy, relaxation methods (transcendental meditation), guided imagery and hypnosis. These methods are even used by many church counselors, coaches, teachers and hospitals, including the most prestigious cancer treatment hospitals, under the name of integrative medicine. It is spiritual, but definitely not Holy Spiritual.

:: An overview of the Spiritist worldview
This worldview also rejects the God of Scripture, but does believe in spirits and demons that dwell in the spirit world. The goal of the Spiritist is to please the

spirits. Wicca is a big part of this movement. Harry Potter is steeped in Spiritism, but is accepted, even by many Christians, because it purportedly stimulates creative thinking and encourages young children to read. Television shows like Charmed and Crossing Over deal with those who are immersed in a Spiritist movement. Truth is found through a Shaman, a medium, who serves as the liaison between humans and the spirit world. The Spiritist believes that "It" created the universe and everything in it, including the spirits. The mess in this world is a result of less advanced, imperfect spirits trying to incite the human beings in which they dwell to do evil. The hope a Spiritist has ultimately comes through a process of moving from being spiritual to a state of spiritual perfection. Their purpose in life is to be spiritually perfected through reincarnation. Upon death the Spiritist is continually reincarnated. Talk about pure hopelessness!

I had to ask myself and you should also: "Which worldview answers the life questions with reason, truth and proof?" If you are undecided, I would encourage you to further study these different worldviews.

I can honestly say that as a result of my studies I have found conclusively that the Christian worldview is more than just a feel-good emotional response to life. It is a belief system that can, and should be, defended in our culture. It is critical that we become intimately familiar with the truth of Christianity, so that we will recognize and respond to the many false claims leveled at Christianity. We also must be able to communicate truths of the biblical worldview to those who believe differently than we do, but do it with love, gentleness, humility and respect. :: :: ::

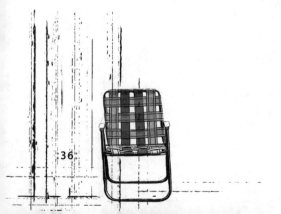

the book or THE BOOK ::

chapter 2

:: **What God?**

we all know that there are a multitude of religious books which claim to have the inside track on God. I found it extremely confusing to figure out what book, if any, was a book of truth. Can anyone know, within a reasonable doubt, that the Bible is reliable and written by God? If the Bible is true, then I can know about God as well as find answers about life and death that I need if I am to build a worldview based on truth. Could it be that God inspired the writing of this book, the Bible?

I was recently addressing a group of seniors in high school who had grown up in an evangelical Bible-believing church. Most of them claimed to be born again and have been baptized. I asked them this question: "If I were an atheist and asked you to give me a reason for why I should consider reading the Bible, what would you say?" A few hands went up.

"Because it is God's Word!" shouted a self-assured student from the front row.

"Really?" I said. "How do you know for sure that it is God's Word?"

The once confident student quietly replied, "Because my parents told me so?"

I then asked, "What happens if your parents are wrong? Might there be other parents out there that are telling their children that the Koran is the only religious book that is true? Might there be a good chance that unless the reliability of the Scriptures can be proven to be the work of God, then Christianity is a hoax, and we have all been fools to have studied and to have followed its teachings?" They became quiet.

Another student who was convinced that she had solved the question piped up. "It takes faith to believe that the Bible is true!"

"Sounds spiritual, but faith in what?" I asked her. "Faith in your opinions or feelings?"

"No," she replied, "just faith."

"It sounds to me that you are saying that for me to believe I would have to commit intellectual suicide, because there is no evidence to prove the truth of the Bible. Is the object of your faith a book, or is it in knowing how the Bible was written, what makes it unique and why man could not, on his own, have written it?" In all my years of teaching and speaking to young adults, I have never, except for my 8-year-old nephew, Frankie Dame, had anyone give me a solid reason for the hope that they had in the reliability of the Scriptures.

For the Christian, all roads lead to the Bible. If the Bible is true and inspired by God, Himself, then everything about the Christian faith can be trusted (Ephesians 3:2-6). If the Bible is authentic, then the following is true also: the Bible is our primary source for learning and understanding life. We can believe the story of creation, the history of Israel, and God's preservation of the Messianic line leading to Christ; all of this is found in the Old Testament. We can also know that the New Testament is the exact account of the fulfillment of all the Messianic prophecies in the Old Testament coming to fruition in the Messiah, the person of Jesus Christ. God ordained the writings in Scripture from the time of Moses to the final writings of the Apostles and Paul in the New Testament, so that we could know Him and understand from where we came, why the world is in such a mess, the hope that we have in Jesus, our purpose in life and what happens when we die. It is the single most important apologetic (proof) that the Christian must know so he can communicate such truths to others.

If, however, the Bible is merely a collection of stories and man's idea of what God might look like, then we are all misinformed and should reject all of it. In this world of Postmodernism, many embrace the idea that absolute truth does not exist. (This, by the way, is an absolute in itself!) Sadly, today, many churches and Christians embrace this notion, and as a result, have a pick and choose mentality when it comes to Scripture. They believe some of it, but not all of it. They might believe that God had a role in creation, but did not create. They believe in Jesus as their Savior, but others can be Christians without believing in Jesus. It is this misdirected theology that has caused much confusion in the church today.

I grieve for the person who comes to church to learn about God because, like me and so many others, they know the way they are living is not filling that giant hole in their heart. They go to church because they want to learn truth, but are instead often fed the worldly philosophy of "just be a good person" or "just be happy" or "give your money and God will heal you and bless you with material wealth." Many so called seeker-friendly churches have watered down the biblical messages because they are afraid of offending someone. These churches entertain their attendees and stay away from talking about truth that might cause tension. However, this tension is what ultimately ushers one into an authentic relationship with the person of Jesus Christ. Instead, these churches are more concerned that no one leaves upset. For many who are seeking God, sadly, they would be better off just staying at home.

The church I attended when I began my search to see if the Bible was true was that kind of a church. It was, and still is, filled with wonderful people and an outgoing, compassionate minister who was, as it turned out to be, sincerely misled. After becoming a believer in Jesus, I asked him why he didn't preach the truth about the need to have a personal relationship with Jesus Christ. He told me that if he preached that "kind of thing, people would leave the church." I shudder for those ministers, pastors and teachers who mislead others in regards to the truths of the Scriptures and Jesus. They will some day have to give account to God, Himself, for the way they lead their people (James 3:1; 2 Corinthians 4:8,10).

In light of all this, allow me to show you the beauty and truth of the Bible. You can trust it to be true. The Bible is a gift from God that confirms His faithfulness, love and sovereignty. The following paragraphs are some of what I found in my search to uncover the truth about the Scriptures. I will be forever indebted to Josh McDowell for his extensive research in this area, as reflected in his book, "Evidence That Demands a Verdict."[1]

Is the Bible reliable? Can we prove the Bible is the Word of God? Could man, without God, have written the Bible? If it is reliable, then all mankind can find meaning and direction for their lives. We no longer have to rely on our own insight into life, but can know for sure that Jesus is the way, the truth and the life. By reading the Scriptures and being inspired by the Holy Spirit, we will come to a deeper understanding about God, and the promise of eternal salvation through His Son, Jesus Christ.

Knowing for sure that the Bible is the Word of God is a critical component in building a Christian worldview. The Bible is the foundation for all that we believe to be true about God, the Holy Spirit and the person of Jesus Christ. Any doubts that you have about your faith, or questions that others have about Christianity can and should be traced back to the Word of God. Pay attention to the truths taught in this lesson and learn how to communicate their authenticity. These truths will not only help you grow in your own faith in God, but will also equip you to always be prepared to give the answer to everyone who asks you the reason for the hope that you have in Jesus Christ, with gentleness and respect (1 Peter 3:15-16).

How do we know it's true? What does God have to say about Scripture? God is claiming authorship over Scripture.

2 Timothy 3:16-17 All Scripture is God-breathed and is useful for teaching, rebuking, correcting and training in righteousness, so that a man of God may be thoroughly equipped for every good work.

2 Peter 1:20-21 Above all, you must understand that no prophecy of Scripture came about by the prophet's own interpretation. For prophecy never had its origin in the will of man, but men spoke from God as they were carried along by the Holy Spirit.

:: Uniqueness of Scripture

As we look into how the Bible was put together, few would disagree that it is the most unique compilation of books ever written. The Bible has been translated into more languages than any other book, and is the most widely circulated book in the world. It is the most extensively read and influential book in history. It has survived throughout the ages, despite its immeasurable opposition. The Bible contains a total of 66 books, 39 of them in the Old Testament and 27 are in the New Testament. The amazing thing about Scripture is that throughout all 66 books there is one theme: the redemption of man through the Messiah, Jesus Christ.

The uniqueness of the Bible is incredible and shows how God wanted to relate and speak to men and women of all ages, professions, cultures and conditions. Consider that it was written over a time span of 1,500 years, 40 generations and by 40 different authors from all walks of life. The Bible reflects the different, sometimes extreme, moods of the writers, as some wrote from great joy to deep sorrow, and at times, paralyzing fear. It was written on three continents: Asia, Europe and Africa. It was written in three languages: Hebrew, Aramaic and Greek. Keep in mind that this was before computers and telephones.

These were men writing what the Holy Spirit was prompting them to write, rather than man's own collaborative efforts. Would it not have been less cumbersome for God to have just dictated His words through one prophet and been done with it? Why did He take 1,500 years and all of those people to write it? God could have just made it appear. But He didn't. He chose to use real people that were far from perfect and very different from each other, so that we could relate personally to the writers and their personalities, as they were writing through the inspiration of the Holy Spirit. Over and over again, God chooses the "lowest of these" to do the great things of God. The same is true today, as He has chosen you and me to go, just as we are, into our own culture and be lights speaking truth into the hearts and minds of those wanting to know truth.

There is so much more to be said about this book. It is simple, yet so profound, that it can be studied for a lifetime and still not be exhausted. The Bible is also unique in that, unlike cults and other false religions, it is not an account of man's efforts to find God, but rather, an account of God's effort to reveal Himself to man. It contains precisely the things that God wants man to know, in exactly the form that He wants us to know them. What an awesome God we worship!

The amazing uniqueness of the Bible, however, does not make it true. How then can we prove that the Bible is true?

> **Katherine's Story.** I was one of the many students who came to Anchorsaway with years of Sunday school and youth group experience under my belt. If you had asked me if I believed the Bible was completely true, I would have said, "Yes, definitely!" If you asked me who wrote the Bible, I would have said, "It was inspired by God. God wrote it through men." Then, you would ask how I know that and I would probably have said something like, "Well, it says in the Bible that it is the true Word of God. I believe that it is true and it has changed my life." I am very pleased to say that, since then, my understanding of the reliability of Scripture has been deepened and broadened.
>
> I learned the big picture of the Bible, how it was written, and how it is different than any other book ever written. I found it fascinating to learn about the discipline, pain and care that was taken for every letter, of every word, on every page, as scribes meticulously copied text to share and preserve the story of God and His people. As I learned about the connections between the Old and New Testaments, I began to see the Bible as a whole story that would be incomplete without all parts. My faith grew as I came to understand that the prophecies found in Isaiah and throughout the Old Testament point clearly to Jesus of the New

Testament. He fulfilled every prophecy concerning the coming Messiah in His life, death and resurrection. It was exciting to learn the real evidence behind my belief that Jesus Christ is the Messiah. I am much more confident in my faith now that I know that it is backed up with solid evidence. I no longer have to live with the uncertainty that comes with belief in something based on "tradition" or "doing what Christians do." Knowing this helped solidify my understanding, and allowed me to make my faith my own and confidently share what I know with those who are searching.

God has used Scripture, even a verse that I have read hundreds of times, to speak to my heart a new way, in a way that relates to where I am and what I am feeling at that very moment. Only God could have written this book. It is unlike any other book on the planet. It is an anchor for my faith. When times get tough and I begin to doubt some of the basic truths of the Christian faith, I can go back and see how the Bible is truly written by God, and that, as a result, God is in control and wants the best for me, whether I can experience Him in that moment or not.

:: Proofs for biblical reliability

According to Josh McDowell, there are three proofs for the reliability of the Bible: bibliographical test, internal evidence test and the external evidence test. We will begin with the bibliographical test, which examines the original manuscripts of the Old and New Testaments to determine how they have been handed down to us. This includes the study of the methods that the Jews used to copy the manuscripts, as well as manuscript comparison.

:: Bibliographical test: the scribes

The scribes, meaning counters, followed strict disciplines regarding the writing of the Scriptures. They wrote with meticulous care and insisted on following conditions that, by today's standards, seem unfathomable.

The text must be written on the skin of a clean animal.

The scroll was prepared for use in synagogue only by a Jew.

It was fastened together with strings from a clean animal.

Each skin contained a specified number of columns, equal throughout the entire book.

The length of each column must extend no less than 48 lines and no more than 60 lines.

The breadth of each column must consist of exactly 30 letters.

Each scribe must use a specially prepared recipe of black ink.

An authentic copy of the text must serve as the example for each scribe to follow.

The scribes were to copy nothing from memory.

The space between every consonant could be no more than the width of a thread.

The breadth between every section must be the same as that of nine consonants.

Between every book was the width of three lines.

The Pentateuch must terminate exactly with a line.

Copyists were required to sit in full Jewish dress.

There was an absolute reverence for the Scripture and the name of God, such that a fresh quill was used each time the sacred name of God was penned. Nothing could interrupt a scribe while writing God's name, not even the presence of a king!

The scribes must produce a master copy.[2]

God wanted to make sure that His Word was copied accurately because God is a God of order and perfection. When I see the care that He ordained the scribes to use in their writing, I am amazed once again at our God and His desire that we know the truth!

:: Bibliographical test: comparison studies

The second bibliographical test compares accepted books of antiquity with one another, in regards to the number of copies of the document and the time span from when the original document was written to the earliest copy that we have today. What is the comparison between the New Testament and other ancient historical writings?

Many of us have read the writings of Caesar, Plato, Socrates and Aristotle and believed them to be accurate as written. Take for example, the author Plato. His writings were done between 427-347 BC with the earliest copy being AD 900. This leaves the time span of 1,200 years with only seven copies surviving since that time. Aristotle has 49 copies in the time span of 1,400 years from the earliest copy. Of all the ancient Greek and Latin literature, Homer's Iliad, as a work of antiquity, possesses the greatest amount of manuscript testimony. It was written in 900 BC, with the earliest copy 400 BC, and the number of existing copies 643. When we compare the New Testament with that of other ancient texts, we find that it was written between AD 40-100 with the earliest copy AD 125—only 25 years from the original. The New Testament copies number more than 24,000.

Floyd McElveen has observed in "God's Word, Final, Infallible and Forever," "Even if someone deliberately or by accident amended or corrupted a manuscript, it would be corrected by the many other manuscripts available. To sum up; unless we want to throw a blanket over all of history and say that there is nothing knowable about the past, no history that can be trusted, no Grecian or Roman history, no Aristotle or Plato or Socrates, we had better not make any claims against the historicity and accuracy of the New Testament. The New Testament documents are far more numerous, older, demonstrably more accurate historically, and have been examined by a far greater battery of scholars, both friend and foe, than all the other ancient manuscripts put together. They have met the test impeccably!"[3]

:: Internal evidence test: prophecy

In my search to find whether or not Christianity was true, the personal revelation of fulfilled prophecies became a giant anchor of my growing faith in Christ. If the prophecies in the Scriptures are true, every one of them, then the Book would have had to be inspired by God, Himself. With the Bible being the only holy book of antiquity that has prophecies, all having been fulfilled except for those that are recorded as future events; it has clearly set itself way apart from other religious writings. I have found that when God wants to make a point, He, Himself, makes it. His thumb print is all over His Book. Take the time to examine the facts; I think that you, too, will conclude that it takes much more faith not to believe than it does to believe in God's inspiration of this most remarkable book we call the Bible.

The internal evidence test tries to see if there are any discrepancies in the Bible. What internal evidences exist that support its authenticity? This is where God makes His strongest appeal. This is the area where my faith took root, because there is absolutely no way that man could have done what God has done with prophecy in the Scriptures. It is through this study and understanding of biblical prophecy that many seekers are convinced that God is truly who He says He is.

In all of Scripture, there are more than 2,000 prophecies. There are approximately 333 prophecies pointing to the Messiah. Of those 333, there are 48 prophecies that do not overlap one another; these are called pure prophecies. The question is this: What are the odds of one man fulfilling all 48 prophecies? For anyone to fulfill all 48 biblical prophecies is scientifically absurd. And yet, the Bible reveals that Jesus did just that.

Peter Stoner, in "Science Speaks," studied the probability of one man fulfilling just eight prophecies as listed below.

1. BORN AT BETHLEHEM
Prophecy: "But as for you, Bethlehem Ephrathah, too little to be among the clans of Judah, from you One will go forth for Me to be ruler in Israel. His goings forth are from long ago, from the days of eternity" (Micah 5:2, NAS). 750 BC
Fulfillment: Jesus was born in Bethlehem of Judea (Matthew 2:1; John 7:42).

2. PRECEDED BY MESSENGER
Prophecy: A voice is calling, "Clear the way for the Lord in the wilderness; Make smooth in the desert a highway for our God" (Isaiah 40:3; Malachi 3:1, NAS). 433 BC
Fulfillment: John the Baptist came, preaching in the wilderness of Judea, saying, "Repent, for the kingdom of heaven is at hand" (Matthew 3:1-3, 11:9-10; Luke 1:17; John 1:23, NAS).

3. HE WAS TO ENTER JERUSALEM ON A DONKEY
Prophecy: "Rejoice greatly, O daughter of Zion! Shout in triumph, O daughter of Jerusalem! Behold, your king is coming to you; He is just and endowed with salvation, humble, and mounted on a donkey, even on a colt, the foal of a donkey" (Zechariah 9:9, NAS). 520 BC
Fulfillment: "And they brought it to Jesus, and they threw their garments on the colt, and put Jesus on it. And as He was going, they were spreading their garments in the road" (Matthew 21:6-11; Luke 19:35-36, NAS).

4. BETRAYED BY A FRIEND
Prophecy: "Even my close friend in whom I trusted, who ate my bread has lifted up his heel against me" (Psalm 41:9, 55:12-14, NAS). 300 BC
Fulfillment: Judas Iscariot was the one who betrayed Him (Matthew 10:4, 26:49-50, NAS).

5. SOLD FOR 30 PIECES OF SILVER
Prophecy: "And I said to them, 'If it is good in your sight, give me my wages; but if not, never mind!' So they weighed out thirty shekels of silver as my wages" (Zechariah 11:12, NAS). 520 BC
Fulfillment: Judas Iscariot asked the price of betrayal, and "they weighed out to him thirty pieces of silver" (Matthew 26:15, 27:3, NAS).

6. MONEY TO BE THROWN IN GOD'S HOUSE
Prophecy: "So I took the thirty shekels of silver and threw them to the potter in the house of the Lord" (Zechariah 11:13b, NAS). 520 BC
Fulfillment: "And he threw the pieces of silver into the sanctuary and departed (Matthew 27:5a, NAS). And they counseled together and with the money bought the Potter's field as a burial place for strangers" (Matthew 27:7, NAS).

7. DUMB BEFORE ACCUSERS
Prophecy: "He was oppressed and He was afflicted, yet He did not open His mouth" (Isaiah 53:7, NAS). 700 BC
Fulfillment: "And while He was being accused by the chief priests and elders, He made no answer" (Matthew 27:12, NAS).

8. HANDS AND FEET PIERCED
Prophecy: They pierced my hands and my feet (Psalm 22:16; Isaiah 53:5, NAS). 520 BC
Fulfillment: "And when they came to the place called the Skull, there they crucified Him" (Luke 23:33, NAS).

Peter Stoner continues: We find that the chance that any man might have lived, down to the present time, and fulfilled all eight prophecies is 1 in 10^{17} (or 1 in 100,000,000,000,000,000). Let us try to visualize this chance … Suppose we take 10^{17} silver dollars and lay them on the face of Texas. They will cover all of the state two feet deep. Now, mark one of these silver dollars and stir the whole mass thoroughly, all over the state. Blindfold a man and tell him that he can travel as far as he wishes, but he must pick up one silver dollar and say that this is the right one. What chance would he have of getting the right one? Just the same chance that the prophets would have had of writing these eight prophecies and having them all come true in any one man, from their day to the present time, providing they wrote them in their own wisdom?[4]

When Stoner considers 48 prophecies, he says, "We find the chance that any one man fulfilled all 48 prophecies to be 1 in 10^{157}."[5]

Chuck Missler has also studied the probabilities of one man (Jesus) fulfilling all 48 Old Testament prophecies. Missler says that the probability of one man fulfilling 16 of the 48 prophecies is 1 in 10^{45}. His concept model is a ball of silver dollars with a radius 30 times the distance of the Earth to the Sun. He follows the same idea as Peter Stoner's illustration of the Texas concept model. He also accepts the probability of all 48 prophecies being fulfilled in one man as being one in 10^{157}. There is no concept model for this, because this number is bigger than the human mind can begin to grasp. Thumbprint of God? You decide. You can choose to reject Jesus Christ as the Son of God, but if you do, keep in mind that you are rejecting a fact proven more absolutely than any other in the world.

I have a friend who is a Messianic Jewish rabbi. His name is Jeff and he has come to the Anchorsaway classes to teach a lesson on why it is difficult for the Jews to believe in Jesus. The following is an excerpt from one of his talks:

> **Jeff's Story.** I now come from a family of four generations of Messianic Jews. My parents, however, were both raised in Orthodox Jewish homes. Orthodox are the most observant of the four major Jewish sects. They were taught to keep Kosher and keep the dietary laws. They didn't drive on the Sabbath and so on. As they grew up, they began to encounter Jewish people who had a whole range of beliefs. There were some who practiced a lot, like my parents' families, while others barely practiced anything at all, who rarely went to Synagogue. But, no matter what Jewish people believed, they held one thing in common: Jewish people can't believe in Jesus. If the Jewish person believes in Jesus, he ceases to be Jewish. That was their mindset. Their greatest fear in becoming a Christian was that they would no longer be Jewish.
>
> They grew up in Cincinnati, like I did, and World War II came and my dad got notice that he'd been drafted into the Navy. He went and told my mom, who he was anxious to impress. She told him, "Well, I've already got a boyfriend in the Army and in the Navy." So, he joined the Marine Corps to really impress her.

Orders came and he was sent off to fight the Japanese. While there, he was frightened about what might happen to him and he prayed to God. This was not very common among Jews. Judaism does not teach much about spontaneous prayer. It does not forbid those prayers; you can pray a spontaneous prayer, but the norm is to just pray the prayers in the prayer book. Dad, however, was so frightened that he spoke to God freely and said, "God, if you'll bring me back home safely from the war ... " He tried to think of something that would really impress God. He said, " ... I'll quit smoking!" He figured that God couldn't turn down that deal. He was in one of the bloodiest battles of the war. As a corporal, he had several experiences in which God really did, literally, answer his prayer for safety.

When he got back to Chesapeake Bay, he threw his cigarettes into the bay and figured, "God did his part; now, I've done mine. God and I are even." He went back to Cincinnati and he and Mom got married. Unfortunately, things did not go well for them and they found themselves fighting all the time, but chose to stay together. Jewish divorce was very rare. They were miserable.

One day, a lady came and knocked on the door. Mom was home and she started to share with Mom about prophecies from the Bible. While she was talking, Dad turned to Mom and said, "You were born a Jew; you're going to die a Jew." He told the lady to stay away and if she ever came back he would throw her down the front stairs. The horrified woman left and the Adlers continued to live in their misery.

Things got worse between Mom and Dad. One day Myrtle, the lady who had knocked on the door, was driving in her car when this voice inside spoke to her and said, "Go visit Ruth Adler." And she thought, "That can't be God. He loves me." She was terrified of my dad. But this voice kept speaking to her: "Go visit Ruth Adler." So, she set her house in order and went. She knocked on the door and Mom was thrilled to see her. Mom's only glimmer of hope came to her through reading the Bible. She knew that Abraham, and Isaac, and Jacob, and David, and Daniel, and Isaiah all had personal relationships with God. She had hoped that she, too, could have this kind of relationship with God.

What Myrtle did not know, and what the Holy Spirit did know, was that glimmer of hope had been taken away by Dad. Feeling utterly lost, she had arranged for us two kids to be asleep, and then she was planning to go up on the roof and jump off. She had planned her own suicide for that very day.

There was a knock at the door and it was Myrtle. Mom desperately wanted to talk to her and gladly invited her in. They started going through those prophecies again and Mom prayed to receive the Messiah. Then the question was: "How do we tell Al? Do we tell Al? Will he kill me? Who will do the funeral?" So they prayed. She told my dad what she had done and he didn't kill her! But for the next several years, six years in fact, he did all that he could to harass her. The Holy Spirit, however, had brought about such a change in my mom's heart. The crueler he was toward her, the more she loved him. She knew that love couldn't come from her; it could only come from the Spirit of God. Dad couldn't take it any longer.

One night he said, "Are you going to your prayer group this evening?"

And she said, "Well, I plan to, but I don't have a ride."

"Get your coat. I'll drive you," he said.

This was a shock; he would always do whatever he could to keep her from going, and now he wanted to go for himself. They pulled up in front of the place where this prayer group met and Dad said, "Marty is in there and I would like to go in and talk to him."

Now, Marty was a Messianic Jewish teacher, and had been for about 20 years. Dad hated him. He thought of him as a traitor who turned other Jews into traitors. And now, Dad actually wanted to go in and talk to him. In the meeting room, Marty was praying and everything was quiet. All of a sudden, the door flew open and my big, loud, angry dad stormed through the door. At least that's the way that Marty always thought of him: big, loud, angry Al. He came through the door right at him, and Marty's thought was: Al has finally flipped and he's come to kill me.

Much to his surprise, Dad went up to him and said, "I want to accept Jesus right now. I believe he is the Messiah." My dad had come to understand the truth that he had been exposed to over those six years. He would not listen to the whole thing at one time, but over time, bit by bit, he had heard the prophecies. The Holy Spirit had cut through all the false ideas and showed him that those prophecies that were in his own Jewish Bible were pointing to Jesus. So, no matter what any man says about Jesus, he knew that was God's Word and that Jesus is the Messiah, because of what

God's Word says. He had always thought of Jesus as the God of the Gentiles. It's important to bear in mind that, before Jesus could be the Savior of the world, He had to be the Messiah of the Jews. It is His fulfillment of the prophecies that made Jesus the Jewish Messiah, and that qualified Him to be the Savior of the world. Dad came to understand that. He prayed and received Jesus, Y'shua, and was dramatically changed.

At first, his parents wouldn't speak to my mom. They blamed her for turning their son into a "traitor." But they began to see changes. They began to see that we still lived as Jews. The Gospel does not come complete with a ham and cheese on rye! We were still Jews. They saw this dramatic transformation, and after six years they began to speak to Mom again, and then they, too, eventually became believers. Then, my mom's mom became a believer. And my sisters and my brothers and I became believers. We were Jews who had found our Messiah!

Myrtle is a perfect example of someone who was prepared to speak to Jeff's mom through the eyes of a Jewish person. She did not speak in Christian terms right away, but rather, spoke to the heart of a Jew. Together they studied their way through the Old Testament prophecies which, by the prompting of the Holy Spirit, brought her to the revelation that Jesus Christ was the Messiah. Had Myrtle not been open to following the lead of the Holy Spirit and had she not been prepared to speak truth, the story you just read could not have taken place. I hope and pray that as you learn the truth of the Christian faith, that God will use you, too, and you might someday have the privilege of leading someone to Jesus, Y'shua, The Messiah!

:: Internal evidence: archaeology

In my mind, God could have stopped the chain of evidence with the fulfillment of prophecy. God, however, continues to shout to a deaf world the truth of the Word and the truth of Himself in a multitude of arenas. There is more internal evidence as we look into the science of archaeology. In what ways have the discoveries of archaeology verified the reliability of the Bible? Over the years there have been many criticisms leveled against the Bible concerning its historical reliability. These criticisms are usually based on a lack of evidence. Since the Bible is a religious book, many scholars take the position that it is biased and cannot be trusted, unless we have corroborating evidence from extra-biblical sources. In other words, the Bible is guilty until proven innocent, and a lack of outside evidence places the biblical account in doubt.

This standard is far different from that applied to other ancient documents, even though many, if not most, have a religious element. They are considered to be accurate, unless there is evidence to show that they are not. Although it is not possible to verify every incident in the Bible, the discoveries of archaeology since the mid-1800s have demonstrated the reliability and plausibility of the Bible narrative.

I had a student contact me to tell me that his professor had said that the Bible was not a reliable book of antiquity, because there was no alphabet at the time of Moses. The student's faith was shaken. Yearly, there are new claims by atheists that try to undermine the reliability of the Scriptures. On the surface, they seem to know what they are talking about, but always upon further investigation, they are found to be misled. Was there an alphabet in the time of Moses? Yes! The discovery of the Ebla archive in northern Syria in the 1970s has shown the biblical writings concerning the Patriarchs to be viable. Documents written on clay tablets from around 2300 BC demonstrate that personal and place names in the Patriarchal accounts are genuine. The name "Canaan" was in use in Ebla, a name critics once said was not used at that time and was used incorrectly in the early chapters of the Bible. The word tehom ("the deep") in Genesis 1:2 was said to be a late word demonstrating the late writing of the creation story. Tehom was part of the vocabulary at Ebla, in use some 800 years before Moses. Ancient customs reflected in the stories of the Patriarchs have also been found in clay tablets from Nuzi (Northern Iraq) and Mari (Mesopotamia).

Here are some more evidences of the findings that support biblical reliability that were found by archaeologists:

The Hittites and Solomon: The Hittites were once thought to be a biblical legend, until their capital and records were discovered at Bogazkoy, Turkey. Many thought the biblical references to Solomon's wealth were greatly exaggerated. Recovered records from the past show that wealth in those times was concentrated in the palace, and therefore, Solomon's prosperity was entirely feasible.

King Belshazzar: Another king whose existence was in doubt was Belshazzar, king of Babylon, named in Daniel 5. According to recorded history, the last king of Babylon was Nabonidus. Tablets were found showing that Belshazzar was Nabonidus' son, who served as co-regent in Babylon. Thus, Belshazzar could offer to make Daniel "third highest ruler in the kingdom" (Daniel 5:16), the highest position available, for reading the handwriting on the wall. Here we see the "eye-witness" nature of the biblical record, as is so often brought out by the discoveries of archaeology.[6]

Meredith's Story. During my years at college, I realized the urgent need for the Christian worldview in academic fields, particularly anthropology. I graduated and joined a small archaeological company where most of the people were hard-core atheists or in search of a spiritual path. During a discussion of the accuracy of the Bible, my boss scornfully identified the Bible as a book full of inaccuracies and errors, and my co-worker agreed. Across the room and unable to participate in the conversation, I swelled with frustration. The Bible's accuracy is not up for debate! Any archaeologist should be impressed by the extent of archaeological and documentary evidence that supports the accuracy of the Bible. I continue to discuss these issues with my co-workers and am thankful I have the freedom to share, even if my comments are met with skepticism. Every Christian should be prepared to give a confident defense of the Bible's accuracy and validity, because it is the source of truth in our faith.

:: External evidence

Our final proof for testing the reliability of the Bible comes from the examination of the literature apart from the Bible that confirms its accuracy. Look back at the historical writers during the time period in question. These writers were not believers in Jesus Christ, they were men merely reporting what they knew to be true. As contemporary, outside sources, these writings also confirm the reliability of Scripture.

Eusebius of Caesarea (AD 263–339) – His Ecclesiastical History preserved the writings of Papias, bishop of Hieropolis (AD 130). Papias, a friend of the Apostle John, wrote:

The Elder (Apostle John) used to say this also: "Mark, having been the interpreter of Peter, wrote down accurately all that he (Peter) mentioned, whether sayings or doings of Christ, not, however, in order. For he was neither a hearer nor companion of the Lord; but afterwards, as I said, he accompanied Peter, who adapted his teachings as necessity required, not as though he were making compilation of the sayings of the Lord. So then Mark made no mistake, writing down in this way some things as he (Peter) mentioned them; for he paid attention to this one thing, not to omit anything that he had heard, nor to include any false statement among them."[7]

Flavius Josephus (AD 37-100?) – As a Jewish historian, he wrote one of the most comprehensive histories of the Jewish people, primarily for the benefit of the non-Jewish world. In "The Antiquities of the Jews," he wrote:

> Now there was about this time Jesus, a wise man, if it be lawful to call him a man, for he was a doer of wonderful works – a teacher of such men as receive truth with pleasure. He drew over to him both many of the Jews, and many of the Gentiles. He was [the] Christ; and when Pilate, at the suggestion of the principal men amongst us, had condemned him to the cross, those that loved him at the first did not forsake him, for he appeared to them alive again the third day, as the divine prophets had foretold these and ten thousand other wonderful things concerning him; and the tribe of Christians, so named from him, are not extinct to this day. (18.3.3.)[8]

The Bible is an amazing collection of books, inspired by God and recorded by man. He wanted us to know beyond a shadow of a doubt that the words were inspired by Him. We saw this played out through the different tests of reliability for books of antiquity: Bibliographical, Internal and External tests. We looked at the way it was written, the comparison with other works, the prophecies, and multiple examples of how archaeology supports the biblical account. Can there be any doubt that the Creator of this vast universe and all that is in it is also the author of the greatest Book ever written? It is a work of love from the Creator to us, His creation.

I learned much about the nature of God as I studied the evidence of the trustworthiness of this book of antiquity. God cares that we know truth. He says in John 14:6-7 "Jesus answered, 'I am the way and the truth and the life. No one comes to the Father except through me. If you really knew me, you would know my Father as well. From now on, you do know him and have seen him.' " Jesus wants us to know Him as being the only truth. He is truth. Why would I rely on man to tell me the answers to life and to God? He has shown Himself to be a God of order, as evidenced by the care He took to make sure that the Old Testament Scriptures were copied by the Scribes. He showed us His all-knowingness (omniscience) through the writings of the prophecies. Perhaps the best part of realizing that the Bible is reliable and can be trusted to be the Word of God Himself, is that we have a guide for living. I no longer had to worry, "What if the Bible is not the truth?"

Perhaps the best way to summarize the Bible is to say that God invites each one of us to read, study and learn from the Truth giver and then, through the inspiration of the Holy Spirit, live out the truths that are found within its covers. He encourages us to give this Book the highest authority in our personal lives, and to use it as our instruction manual for living life to its full and for impacting our culture for Christ.

John 8:31-32 To the Jews who had believed him, Jesus said, "If you hold to my teaching, you are really my disciples. Then you will know the truth, and the truth will set you free."

I encourage you to check out other religions' books and see if there is fulfilled prophecy. I did, and it was at that point in my life that God confirmed to me that He is who He said He is, and I could stake my life on it … He did. :: :: ::

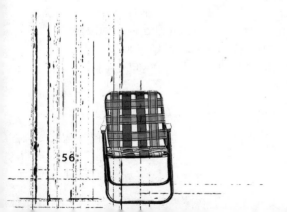

ROAD BLOCKS ::

Photo by Stacey Kish, www.flickr.com/photos/javanutmom

chapter 3

:: **What God?**

one of my favorite places to go is to the theatre. I love the whole thing: the bustling crowds finding and settling in their seats, the orchestra music, the blackout, excitement as the curtain goes up and the play begins in full living color! I have great admiration for those who have the gift of acting; how they can throw themselves night after night into their character is an amazing feat. When the performance comes to a close, the curtain comes down, the cast takes a final curtain call, the crowd applauds, and we, the spectators, are gently taken from the fantasy of the stage back into the real world.

I can only imagine what it must have been like to go to the theatre in Jesus' day. Wonderful amphitheaters carved into hills, seats of natural wood, grass or stone and perfect acoustics from the stage to the seats. It was the custom for the Greek and Roman actors to speak using masks with a device in them that would magnify their voices.[1] Jesus, no doubt, was very familiar with the theatre, as it was a significant part of the culture. I find it interesting that the Greek word for actor is *hupokrites* from where we get the word hypocrite. It means "an actor under an assumed character" (stage-player).[2] Jesus referred to the hypocrites several times in Scripture, because it painted for those who listened to Him a perfect picture of the type of person that we should not become. The Gospel writers had much to say about hypocrites.

John 8:1-11 But Jesus went to the Mount of Olives. At dawn he appeared again in the temple courts, where all the people gathered around him, and he sat down to teach them. The teachers of the law and the Pharisees brought in a woman caught in adultery. They made her stand before the group and said to Jesus, "Teacher, this woman was caught in the act of adultery. In the Law Moses commanded us to stone such women. Now what do you say?" They were using this question as a trap, in order to have a basis for accusing him.

But Jesus bent down and started to write on the ground with his finger. When they kept on questioning him, he straightened up and said to them, "If any one of you is without sin, let him be the first to throw a stone at her." Again he stooped down and wrote on the ground.

At this, those who heard began to go away one at a time, the older ones first, until only Jesus was left, with the woman still standing there. Jesus straightened up and asked her, "Woman, where are they? Has no one condemned you?"

"No one, sir," she said.

"Then neither do I condemn you," Jesus declared. "Go now and leave your life of sin."

Matthew 23:25-26 (Jesus speaking) "Woe to you, teachers of the Law and Pharisees, you hypocrites! You clean the outside of the cup and dish, but inside they are full of greed and self-indulgence. Blind Pharisee! First clean the inside of the cup and dish, and then the outside also will be clean."

Why is it that you or your friends might choose not to attend church or have anything to do with Christianity? I believe that one of the most common reasons why most people do not believe in Christ or attend a church is, in their words, because "it's filled with hypocrites." Obviously, not all Christians are hypocrites, pretending to be someone that they are not, but most would agree that this is a problem in the majority of churches. I had a student last year who stopped coming to Anchorsaway because the girls in her small group were friendly and loving on Sunday night, but would not talk to her at school. I can't imagine just how many "religious" people turn a cold shoulder to those who are different from them outside of the church setting, and in return these victims turn a cold shoulder to God.

Yes, we all sin and those who believe in Christ, although forgiven, must continually keep themselves in check (1 John 1:9), so as to be a light to those living in darkness. With all that said, many Christians feel like they must pretend to have it all together, seeming to live moment by moment a "happy" life. They would like to make others think that they never struggle and certainly would never doubt their faith. Their choice of speech is generally one of condescension mixed with arrogance. They are quick to tell "their story," but are slow to listen to others. What is it about these people that draw people to Christ? Regrettably, not much.

Imagine, for just a moment, what would happen if Christians committed to being honest and real about their struggles, doubts, fears and questions? Just think of Christians breaking free from their holy huddles and reaching out as true friends to those whom God has put in their lives, who just need someone who is real with whom to talk and share their lives.

Have you ever felt pressure from your church or other Christians that your life must, at least on the outside, appear to be perfect with no doubts or fears?

Truth is, we all have periods of doubt and questions when it comes to life, God, the future and the purpose of living in a broken and hurting world. No human being has all the answers; we're not supposed to. If we did, we would be God ourselves! God wants us to seek Him so that He can quiet our minds and our hearts with His peace.

Deuteronomy 4:29-30 But if from there you seek the LORD your God, you will find him if you look for him with all your heart and with all your soul. When you are in distress and all these things have happened to you, then in later days you will return to the LORD your God and obey him.

Matthew 7:7-8 (Jesus speaking) "Ask and it will be given to you; seek and you will find; knock and the door will be opened to you. For everyone who asks receives; he who seeks finds; and to him who knocks, the door will be opened."

As healthy as it can be to doubt, it is extremely unhealthy to push that doubt or our questions away. Gone unresolved, our personal doubts, fears and questions can make us bitter, angry and, often times, depressed. For us to become spiritually, mentally and emotionally healthy, it is good to process all of our "stuff" against the back drop of the One who is eternal and true.

Philippians 4:4-7 Rejoice in the Lord always. I will say it again: Rejoice! Let your gentleness be evident to all. The Lord is near. Do not be anxious about anything, but in everything, by prayer and petition, with thanksgiving, present your requests to God. And the peace of God, which transcends all understanding, will guard your hearts and your minds in Christ Jesus.

Several years ago, my son, Mark, came into my office one evening and said, "What happens if I can't believe? I just can't make myself believe. I honestly doubt everything about God. I want to believe God, but I just can't." I was touched that he would admit his feelings about his faith, and furthermore want to talk about it. I assured him that his kind of doubt was a good thing and, in the end, it would draw him closer to God, thus increasing his faith. I told him that God honors honest seekers and that Mark should always feel free to ask questions and then seek out answers from trusted people or sources. I assured him that God has a plan for him that is special and unique. I encouraged him to read a little of the book Ephesians each day. By the end of our conversation, he was going to try reading the Bible, praying and looking for the ways God was working in his life that he was overlooking. For him, the best thing that came out of our conversation was that he knew that it was OK to doubt, and that God would meet him right where he was. We prayed together, asking God to increase his faith. Not surprisingly, God has been faithful to Mark!

Jessica was a student of mine who attended a Christian school for eight years and graduated first in her class. As a high school senior, she appeared to have everything together, as she was an extremely bright and talented young lady who loved God and life. She decided to attend a secular college in order to reach out to nonbelievers. She was not as prepared as she thought she was, but God was not about to let her go!

> **Jessica's Story.** The past two years of my life in college have been very full—full of asking questions, seeking answers, confronting challenges, experiencing change—in a word, a time of growth. And growing, I've found, is both uncomfortable and irresistible.
>
> The fall semester of my freshman year, however, went differently than expected. I was able to talk about Jesus with girls on my floor, and I enjoyed seeking out relationships with some of the overlooked students on our campus, especially some international students. I also got involved in a Christian fellowship, which provided a familiar source of encouragement to me when I felt too far from home. What I did not anticipate, however, was the way my own faith would be so strongly challenged in just the first two months of my college career. I saw professors and students who considered the God of the Bible to be no more than one of many acceptable moral theories, and I began to question the validity of my own faith.
>
> For a whole year, I was frustrated by plaguing doubts, and I longed for the certainty I saw in other dedicated Christians. Some of the most exciting spiritual conversations I had during the course of that year were with students questioning or seeking God. I was able to relate to their uncertainty, and encouraged them to ask God to reveal His truth personally.
>
> I found it amazing that even when I had nagging doubts, or felt that my faith was weak and that my abilities were lacking, God still used me in ministry. When I felt the most incapable, I became willing to listen to His

direction. I believed that God was encouraging me to start a Bible study in my dorm. By my sophomore year, I participated in outreach events to connect new freshmen to our campus fellowship. God was teaching me that His ability to use me to further His kingdom did not ultimately depend on my knowledge, or capability or preparedness. It was God who was transforming me to be more like Him, and the result was a righteousness that attracts people to Him. God is faithful and I could not be more excited to be His servant!

:: From where did doubt come?

Doubt was first introduced to mankind in the Garden of Eden. It was Satan's goal, then and now, to cause man to take his eyes off of God and onto himself.

Genesis 3:1-6 Now the serpent was more crafty than any of the wild animals the LORD God had made. He said to the woman, "***Did God really say***, 'You must not eat from any tree in the garden'?"

The woman said to the serpent, "We may eat fruit from the trees in the garden, but God did say, 'You must not eat fruit from the tree that is in the middle of the garden, and you must not touch it, or you will die.' "

"You will not surely die," the serpent said to the woman. "For God knows that when you eat of it your eyes will be opened, and you will be like God, knowing good and evil."

When the woman saw that the fruit of the tree was good for food and pleasing to the eye, and also desirable for gaining wisdom, she took some and ate it. She also gave some to her husband, who was with her, and he ate it. (emphasis added)

Did you catch it? Doubt was birthed in the first recorded words of Satan: "Did God really say?" Satan was bringing into question the truth of God, His Word and His character. Satan first questioned the truth of God's statement, and then quickly came up against God, by contradicting God's charge to Eve by offering her something that was appealing and might make her feel good for a time. Because Satan was able to get Eve's heart and mind off of God, she doubted what God had told her and was easily persuaded to disobey Him. Satan added to her doubt by promising her that she could be "like God," meaning becoming like God herself. "Satan quickly suggested that man's great desire to be equal to and truly like God, had been deliberately thwarted by divine command. He charged the Creator with selfishness and with a malicious falsehood, representing Him as envious and unwilling for His creatures to have something that would make them like the omniscient One."[3]

The irony about this statement is that it was Satan's own desire to be God and that is what got him in trouble with God and kicked out of heaven in the first place (Ezekiel 28:11-19; Isaiah 14:12-20; Luke 10:18). If Eve had believed God and obeyed Him, she never would have bitten on Satan's lie. Eve walked and had a relationship with God, Himself. She had it all but still was looking for something more. Why? Satan knew our weakness. He persuaded her, as he continually persuades us, that as great as God is, as much as He loves us, He still withholds from us those things that will make us happy and bring us joy. "Maybe God doesn't want me to be happy. He's a cosmic killjoy. Living for God is nothing more than keeping a bunch of rules and is keeping me from experiencing the fun that the world has to offer." These are all things we say or think as we give in to other temptations.

From the beginning of the Old Testament through the New Testament, Satan desires for us to take our eyes off Jesus and put our trust in our own self effort.

Matthew 14:25-33 During the fourth watch of the night Jesus went out to them, walking on the lake. When the disciples saw him walking on the lake, they were terrified. "It's a ghost," they said, and cried out in fear.

But Jesus immediately said to them: "Take courage! It is I. Don't be afraid."

"Lord, if it's you," Peter replied, "tell me to come to you on the water."

"Come," he said.

Then Peter got down out of the boat, walked on the water and came toward Jesus. But when he saw the wind, he was afraid and, beginning to sink, cried out, "Lord, save me!"

Immediately Jesus reached out his hand and caught him. "You of little faith," he said, "why did you doubt?"

And when they climbed into the boat, the wind died down. Then those who were in the boat worshiped him, saying, "Truly you are the Son of God."

Peter temporarily took his mind and eyes off of Jesus and immediately began to sink. Sounds just like me. When I focus on myself by taking my eyes and mind off of Jesus, I, too, begin to sink. I worry. I get upset when things don't go my way. I am quick to judge others and I become an expert at figuring out how to fix something or somebody that, really, only God can heal. All this to say that when I begin to think that God is not sufficient to do all things and that He needs me to help, doubt takes up residency in my mind and in my heart. I can tell you, it does not lead to peace and joy.

Addressing doubt and questions can be overwhelming and complex, because often, emotions take over. Dealing with unbelief is a process. To be able to claim understanding and victory over doubt takes perseverance and hard work. It is not a quick fix, but those who are willing to allow God to unravel their preconceptions about life, people and God Himself will become people who, in the midst of their circumstances, will have a peace and a joy that they never knew existed.

:: Stubborn doubt

There are different types of doubt. One is a stubborn doubt that says, "No matter what you say, no matter what evidence says, I choose not to believe in God in any way, shape or form." One who willfully chooses not to believe is one who is outwardly satisfied, but is not at peace in his or her state of doubt or unbelief. They make no effort to find truth that could relieve their doubt, but rather, in their stubbornness, they choose to live their lives contrary to God and His Word. Sadly, for many, they will miss the very thing they are looking for when they turn a deaf ear to God. The stubborn doubter reminds me of G.K. Chesterton's words when he said, "The problem with Christianity is not that it has been tried and found wanting, but that it has been found difficult and left untried."

Be reminded that God is a loving God who is calling all, even the stubborn doubter, to Himself. God will never stop loving them. If someone chooses to refuse the call from God, He will give them the desire of their heart. This should alarm the willful skeptic or cynic; God will never force Himself into your life, nor will He force you to love Him. However, for those who choose to be stubborn, the door is open for them to change their mind and to come to Him. God will not refuse them; He loves those who repent and receive His love and forgiveness. For those who choose to remain closed to God through stubbornness, God has a word for them. The obstinate person is addressed in the following Scriptures:

James 1:5-8 If any of you lacks wisdom, he should ask God, who gives generously to all without finding fault, and it will be given to him. But when he asks, he must believe and not doubt, because he who doubts is like a wave of the sea, blown and tossed by the wind. That man should not think he will receive anything from the Lord; he is a double-minded man, unstable in all he does.

Psalm 81:12 (The Psalmist quoting the God of Jacob) "So I gave them over to their stubborn hearts to follow their own devices."

There is nothing healthy or productive about being stubborn and closed to God. How sad that those who have turned away from truth, have turned also away from life and from life everlasting. Pray for them that God would not harden their hearts to Him, and that, as an act of their will, they would turn to God who is waiting for them!

:: Reasonable doubt

As much as God hates a stubborn heart, He loves the one who has doubts and questions, and is not afraid to face and to work through them. Some who doubt have unanswered questions that need answering. These people are seekers that, quite simply, want to know more and do not know where to go for answers. God encourages this and tells us in Scripture to "test all things and hold on to that which is good" (1 Thessalonians 5:21).

Most of us have doubts of the mind. For example, we just can't imagine how Jesus could have been brutally beaten and killed on a cross, then put in a tomb with a giant boulder rolled in front of it, and then three days later, poof, there was Jesus walking around. It makes no sense, people die and stay dead. It just could not have happened; it must be another fable. However, when one digs into the writings of authors who lived at the time of Christ, the seeker will find verification in many books of antiquity that the Bible is true beyond a reasonable doubt.

Many have set out to disprove the writings of Scripture and have found as a result of their massive research, that what was recorded in Scripture was true. D. James Kennedy wrote in his book "Why I Believe" about many brilliant thinkers who challenged the truth of the Scriptures, and ended up believing after they examined the historical evidence. One such person was Sir Cecil Wakeley, one of the world's leading scientists whose credentials are rather impressive – K.B.E., C.B., LL.D., M.CH., Doctor of Science, F.R.C.S., and past president of Royal College of Surgeons of Great Britain. He said, "Scripture is quite definite that God created the world, and I for one believe that to be a fact, not fiction. There is no evidence, scientific or otherwise, to support the theory of evolution."

Oftentimes, doubts of the mind can be satisfied by studying the word of God, reading reliable outside resources, and talking with men and women who have Godly wisdom. In James 1:5-7, God makes it very clear that if you ask for wisdom, He will give it to you, abundantly!

:: Heartfelt doubt

There are also doubts of the heart and emotions which cannot be satisfied through reading and studying. These doubts come from those who are deeply suffering, and only God Himself can quiet a broken heart. Ravi Zacharias, in his book "Cries of the Heart," writes about "a man who had come from a country where much blood had been spilled in internal strife, a land where someone's heart was broken every day by some stray bullet, or a hate-filled ideological conflict. He told me that even though, for years, he had found comfort in the knowledge that Christ had borne his sins, it was new realization, years later, when he took note that Christ had borne our sorrows, too."

"That intimacy with God is a knowledge that bridges what one knows with what one feels. Such knowledge takes what we know and what we feel seriously. This is not a fatalistic posture that says, 'So be it,' resigned to accept what flies in the face of reason. When we learn God's profound answers to every sentiment we feel, we find contentment and courage, and live a life of hope and confidence. We then make every day count with significance, while treasuring His thoughts and harnessing our feelings."

Know that God wants to quiet your heart. No matter who you are, or what you have done, or have gone through, God is there with you and for you. He wants you to know Him, to learn from Him and to talk to Him. You matter a great deal to God; He died for you, not only so that your sins are forgiven and that you might have eternal life, but also that He might have a relationship with you that is real, that will give you life, hope, joy and peace.

Revelation 3:20-22 (Jesus speaking) "Here I am! I stand at the door and knock. If anyone hears my voice and opens the door, I will come in and eat with him, and he with me. To him who overcomes, I will give the right to sit with me on my throne, just as I overcame and sat down with my Father on his throne. He who has an ear, let him hear what the Spirit says to the churches."

I am closing this chapter by sharing with you two specific times that God spoke to me about specific doubts that I had as a new believer. I hope that they will encourage you in your spiritual quest.

I was frustrated because nothing made sense to me, to the point that I would often think that God was playing with my mind. One day, I was walking into a baseball game (late, of course), and there on the outside of the stadium, were some boys who were peeking through a crack in the fencing that was surrounding the field. They were having a ball taking turns looking through the hole even though their view was limited. The realization of what was happening hit me like a ton of bricks as I entered the stadium and sat in my seat. We could see the whole picture: the players, the umpires, the scoreboard and the game, itself. The boys on the outside, peeking in, must have had a very limited and distorted picture of what was actually happening on the inside. I understood for the first time, that much of my own frustration about life and people was because I had such a limited view of life and eternity. I was seeing life with a finite mind, and did not and could not see life from God's perspective. For me, it was a turning point in my faith. I needed to be content in what I did know and understand, and to be joyful in what God did show me. The more I learned about our infinite and sovereign God, the more my faith grew and doubts diminished.

Another time of struggle and doubt for me was the security of my own salvation. I believed that Christ is God and that He died for my sins and rose again. No question about it. What I was not sure of was God's acceptance of my faith in Him. My mind was set, but my heart was far away. I was unsure that if I died I would go to heaven. I thought about this all the time and it was affecting my personal growth in my faith. I would pray any prayer of salvation any and every time it was offered. Sometimes when I was asked to speak and, at the end, give people a chance to give their lives to Christ, I would pray right along with those whom I was leading in prayer. This was literally driving me crazy, and I needed some Godly counsel.

I sought guidance from a good friend, Anne Walls, who is one of the smartest and most Godly women I knew. She told me that Satan was behind this in that he was successfully distracting me from my trusting Christ. Her advice was life changing to me and to the many that I have shared it with since. She said that there are times when we simply must choose to believe, in spite of what our emotions are telling us. She suggested to me that my faith should not just be an emotional response to Christ, but rather, a commitment built on the truth of the Word of God. I needed to fight back with Scripture and a truth statement. From that time on, whenever I got those doubt thoughts about my salvation, I quoted John 3:16, 17 and said, "Thank You, Lord, for making me Your child because of my faith in You. Thank You for promising never to leave me. Thank You for assuring me that when I die, I will go to heaven to be with You! Amen." From that moment on, whenever I thought that I was not His, I went through my routine. At the beginning, I went through it several times a day. As the days passed, I did it less and less, and in about three or four weeks, I no longer had any doubt about my salvation. If you struggle with certain truths of God, try this exercise and hopefully you, too, will overcome your doubts of your heart.

Whether it is stubborn, reasonable or heartfelt doubt, God wants to meet you right where you are now! He promises that if you look for Him, you will find Him. Where should you look? Your answers will be found in the Scriptures, in prayer and through friends who are wise and living out their faith. Remember that God is faithful and wants you to have true peace and joy. If you seek, you will find. No doubt about it! :: :: ::

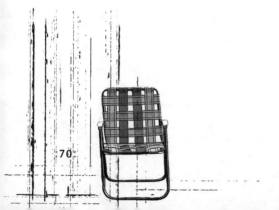

DEAD OR ALIVE ::

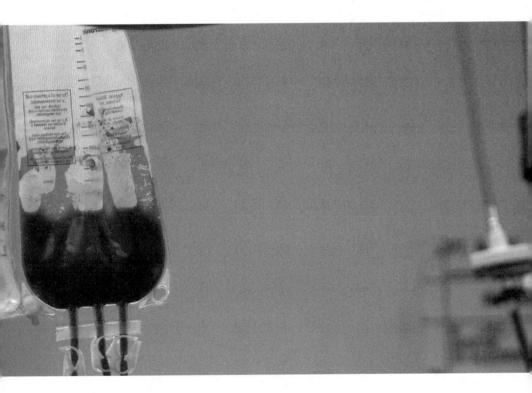

chapter 4

i remember a camping trip that our family took up into Maine. We had our van packed to the brim with enough gear to spend weeks in the wilderness. Our kids were all teenagers and were lukewarm about the whole camping idea. None of us had a voice in the decision but Ed, who, being an Eagle Scout, thought it would be great for us to experience nature in nature. As we were eating boiled lobster, which I must admit was the best that I have ever tasted, there were bets from Scott, Mark and Andrew as to who would get scared and end up sleeping in the van. All claimed to be brave and courageous. They convinced each other that there was no creature big or mean enough that would scare them. We closed down camp, Ed told one of his ghost stories, and our daring warriors settled down in their tents. Kelly made no such claims of bravery and insisted on sleeping in our tent. I waited until everyone was sleeping, grabbed my pillow, and slept well on the foldout couch in the van. In the morning I woke up, and to my surprise, Kelly and my brave warriors were all sound asleep next to me.

Have you ever made promises of bravado? Anyone can make a claim. We all can avow to be courageous, but when hard times come to prove our unwavering courage, all of us, at one time or another, fail the test. Some of us claim to have faith, but so often when difficult times come, we find our faith has shifted from trusting Christ to work things out, to trusting ourselves in spite of God. There was only one man who made a claim that only God could keep: that was Jesus. Jesus claimed to be God. Jesus also said that He would be killed, and buried, and rise again in three days. If He could do this, then Jesus Christ is truly God.

What is the one thing that Jesus Christ could do to, once and for all, prove His deity? Back in the Garden of Eden (Genesis 3), Adam and Eve chose to disobey God. The penalty was a physical death (we will all die) and a spiritual death which is separation from having fellowship with God. Adam and Eve had to leave the garden, because God did not want them to eat from the tree of eternal life in their new found fallen state. God wanted to restore them from their sin. In Genesis 3:15, God had promised that there would be a Messiah that would come and defeat Satan. He would pay the penalty for their sins and re-establish an intimate relationship, through the indwelling of the Holy Spirit, with all who believed. How would this happen? Jesus Christ would prove His deity; He would pay, once and for all, the penalty of sin for all mankind by willingly going to the cross, dying and then three days later, coming to life again! That is the Gospel—the good news!

The resurrection of Jesus Christ is the focal point of the Christian faith. It is recorded in Scripture as being the single most important event in the history of mankind and was the culmination of Christ's life on earth.

1 Corinthians 15:1-8 Now, brothers, I want to remind you of the Gospel I preached to you, which you received and on which you have taken your stand. By this Gospel you are saved, if you hold firmly to the word I preached to you. Otherwise, you have believed in vain. For what I received I passed on to you as of first importance: that Christ died for our sins according to the Scriptures, that he was buried, that he was raised on the third day according to the Scriptures, and that he appeared to Peter, and then to the Twelve. After that, he appeared to more than five hundred of the brothers at the same time, most of whom are still living, though some have fallen asleep. Then he appeared to James, then to all the Apostles, and last of all he appeared to me also, as to one abnormally born.

:: Did this really happen?
1 Corinthians 15:12-13, 19 But if it is preached that Christ has been raised from the dead, how can some of you say that there is no resurrection of the dead? If there is no resurrection of the dead, then not even Christ has been raised. And if Christ has not been raised, our preaching is useless and so is your faith ... If only for this life we have hope in Christ, we are to be pitied more than all men.

Strong words from the inspired Apostle Paul—if Christ did not rise from the dead, then Christianity is a complete hoax and those who do believe are to be pitied. If Christ did not rise from the dead, then He wasn't able to conquer death, meaning that death was stronger than Christ and, in turn, stronger than God. If Christ didn't rise from the dead, He was not really God. But this is not the case. From the previous chapter, knowing for certain that Scripture was inspired by God, we can rest assured that if Scripture tells it, then it did happen. Christ rose from the dead!

This is the true story of the death and resurrection of Christ. Be assured that this was no surprise to Christ. He knew forever ago that He would die for the sins of the world. He knew the costs, which we can only imagine, and He even talked about it with His disciples. "'We are going up to Jerusalem,' he said, 'and the Son of Man will be betrayed to the chief priests and teachers of the law. They will condemn him to death and will hand him over to the Gentiles, who will mock him and spit on him, flog him and kill him. Three days later he will rise'" (Mark 10:33-34).

What was it about Jesus that was causing the Jews to be in such an uproar that they would want to kill Him? Scripture again gives us the answer! Jesus asked the people for which miracle they were stoning Him. "We are not stoning you for any of these [miracles]," replied the Jews, "but for blasphemy, because you, a mere man, claim to be God" (John 10:33).

One of the most amazing themes of the life and death of Jesus is the continued compassion that He had, not only for the disciples, but for those who were yet to be born. In the midst of His personal agony, Jesus was praying for you when He was in the Garden of Gethsemane. What does this tell you about the heart of God?

John 17:20-26 (Jesus speaking) "My prayer is not for them alone. I pray also for those who will believe in me through their message, that all of them may be one, Father, just as you are in me and I am in you. May they also be in us so that the world may believe that you have sent me. I have given them the glory that you gave me, that they may be one as we are one: I in them and you in me. May they be brought to complete unity to let the world know that you sent me and have loved them even as you have loved me. Father, I want those you have given me to be with me where I am, and to see my glory, the glory you have given me because you loved me before the creation of the world. Righteous Father, though the world does not know you, I know you, and they know that you have sent me. I have made you known to them, and will continue to make you known in order that the love you have for me may be in them and that I myself may be in them."

What a beautiful, loving, tender-hearted, courageous God we worship! If you have time, go back and feast on the whole chapter of John 17 to learn more about the heart of our Lord.

Jesus finished praying and soon one of Jesus' best friends, Judas, came into the garden. Jesus even had Judas sitting at his right side, the place of honor, during the Last Supper. He loved Judas, but I am sure that the heart of Jesus was breaking as He knew that Judas had rejected the love that Christ had offered to him. More than disbelief, He had betrayed the Son of God. How it must still break the heart of God, when He looks into the hearts of those whom He created who have also turned away from His offer to love Him.

It was dark in the garden and Jesus must have heard the battalion of probably several hundred men coming up the hill, and seen the reflective light of the torches as they came into the garden to arrest Him. Don't miss this: They were coming to arrest God!

In the midst of all the chaos, Jesus was still showing His deity and loving His own, as well as those who wanted to kill Him. "Jesus, knowing all that was going to happen to him, went out and asked them, 'Who is it you want?' 'Jesus of Nazareth,' they replied. 'I am he,' Jesus said. (And Judas the traitor was standing there with them.) When Jesus said, 'I am he,' they drew back and fell to the ground" (John 18:4-5).

Picture it. All who knew Jesus knew that He did not carry weapons and had never fought anyone. It was not in His nature to do that. Nevertheless, in marched perhaps up to hundreds of fully armed soldiers, along with the "religious" leaders. What happened when Jesus merely spoke His name? They all fell down! Can you imagine what that must have looked like? They picked themselves up off the ground and, once again, asked Jesus who He was. He again confirmed that He was Jesus of Nazareth and then asked that his friends be released. "Then Simon Peter, who had a sword, drew it and struck the high priest's servant, cutting off his right ear. (The servant's name was Malchus.) Jesus commanded Peter, 'Put your sword away! Shall I not drink the cup the Father has given me?'" (John 18:10-11).

I really don't blame Peter, he was simply trying to protect Jesus even though Jesus had specifically told Peter what must happen before even coming to Jerusalem. Peter, himself, was seeing Jesus' words coming to fruition. To get the whole picture, look at what Luke had to say about what happened next.

Luke 22:49-51 When Jesus' followers saw what was going to happen, they said, 'Lord, should we strike with our swords?' And one of them struck the servant of the high priest, cutting off his right ear. But Jesus answered, 'No more of this!' And he touched the man's ear and healed him.

Jesus, the God-man, touched the man's ear and he was healed. This healed soldier is the same man who fell over upon hearing the name of Jesus, and now he was getting an ear job! You would think that the soldier would have, right then, bowed down to worship Jesus as God! There is no record that he responded in any way to Christ. Isn't it amazing how our biased presuppositions can blind us when we are faced with truth?

After all that had happened with Jesus' revealing to the soldiers His deity, they bound and arrested Him! I am reminded to pray for those in my life who have done the same thing: heard the truth of Jesus, but have not heard a thing because of their own stubbornness. I pray that God would open their hearts and minds to the truth of Himself.

It was Friday and there continued to be many accusations against Christ. He went through six trials, three Roman and three Jewish. Jesus then stood before the governor, Pilate, and made a personal appeal to Pilate about who He was and about His purpose for being on earth (John 18:37-40). Have you ever known people who asked a question, but really didn't want to know the answer? Pilate asked Jesus a question about truth, but immediately walked out to the crowds of people and asked what they wanted done with Jesus. It seemed that Pilate found more comfort in a crowd of people than he did with God. The people wanted Jesus crucified and Pilate was going to give them the desire of their hearts. Trying to play both sides of the fence, Pilate said that he did not think that He was deserving of death, but that he would permit it. Good try, Pilate. Jesus says in Matthew 12:30, "He who is not with me is against me ..." Sitting on the fence when it comes to Jesus is not an option.

With the decision made to kill Jesus, Pilate sent Him to be whipped.

Matthew 27:28-31 They stripped him and put a scarlet robe on him, and then twisted together a crown of thorns and set it on his head. They put a staff in his right hand and knelt in front of him and mocked him. 'Hail, king of the Jews!' they said. They spit on him, and took the staff and struck him on the head again and again. After they had mocked him, they took off the robe and put his own clothes on him. Then they led him away to crucify him.

Once at the cross, the soldiers nailed Jesus' wrists and feet to the cross. He was only two or three feet above the ground, and was at a place where all those coming to celebrate Passover would walk by Him, spit on Him or hurl insults at Him. Did you catch the hypocrisy? Thousands of Jews were coming into the city to celebrate God's mercy that He showed the Jewish nation, and there, right in the midst of the Roman and Jewish crucifixion, hung Jesus, God!

He was given some wine vinegar to drink by someone standing near. "But the rest said, 'Now leave him alone. Let's see if Elijah comes to save him.' Jesus then cried out and gave up his spirit" (Matthew 27:49-50). Sinless Jesus died.

Remember at the beginning of this chapter, you read how Jesus told what was going to happen to Him? It did, just as He said it would. Knowing this, Pilate sent out another Roman guard to guard the tomb. (I have always wondered if Malchus was in that group.) The Romans knew what Jesus had said and had to make sure that no one would steal the body of Jesus, and then tell others that He was resurrected. This would have been a great threat to Pilate and his rule over his kingdom. Little did he know that God's Kingdom was about ready to make quite an entrance!

There were no numbers of guards, a big enough rock or deep enough wounds to keep Jesus in the tomb. It was Sunday morning and He had risen! "Now the first day of the week Mary Magdalene went to the tomb early, while it was still dark, and saw that the stone had been taken away from the tomb" (John 20:1, KJV). The stone had not just been rolled down hill, it had been "airo," which is the Greek word that means "to pick something up and carry it away."[1]

Mark 16:1-8 When the Sabbath was over, Mary Magdalene, Mary the mother of James, and Salome bought spices so that they might go to anoint Jesus' body. Very early on the first day of the week, just after sunrise, they were on their way to the tomb and they asked each other, "Who will roll the stone away from the entrance of the tomb?"

But when they looked up, they saw that the stone, which was very large, had been rolled away. As they entered the tomb, they saw a young man dressed in a white robe sitting on the right side, and they were alarmed.

"Don't be alarmed," he said. "You are looking for Jesus the Nazarene, who was crucified. He has risen! He is not here. See the place where they laid him. But go, tell his disciples and Peter, He is going ahead of you into Galilee. There you will see him, just as he told you."

Trembling and bewildered, the women went out and fled from the tomb. They said nothing to anyone, because they were afraid.

John 20:3-9 So Peter and the other disciple started for the tomb. Both were running, but the other disciple outran Peter and reached the tomb first. He bent over and looked in at the strips of linen lying there but did not go in. Then Simon Peter, who was behind him, arrived and went into the tomb. He saw the strips of linen lying there, as well as the burial cloth that had been around Jesus' head. The cloth was folded up by itself, separate from the linen. Finally the other disciple, who had reached the tomb first, also went inside. He saw and believed. (They still did not understand from Scripture that Jesus had to rise from the dead.)

It is not hard to imagine the sight which greeted the eyes of the Apostles when they reached the tomb: the stone slab, the collapsed grave clothes, the shell of the head-cloth and the gap between the two. No wonder they "saw and believed." A glance at these grave clothes proved the reality, and indicated the nature, of the resurrection. They were like a discarded chrysalis, or cocoon, from which the butterfly has emerged.

Luke 24:9-11 When they came back from the tomb, they told all these things to the Eleven and to all the others. It was Mary Magdalene, Joanna, Mary the mother of James, and the others with them who told this to the Apostles. But they did not believe the women, because their words seemed to them like nonsense.

As a side note, according to Jewish principles of legal evidence, women were invalid. Christ loves men and women alike, and shows no bias to either one, unlike the Jewish law. Isn't it just like Jesus to let the women to be the first to spread the good news, "He has risen!"

Christ's appearances were not only confirmed by the women, but by many others.

1 Corinthians 15:3-8 For what I received I passed on to you as of first importance: that Christ died for our sins according to the Scriptures, that he was buried, that he was raised on the third day according to the Scriptures, and that he appeared to Peter, and then to the Twelve. After that, he appeared to more than five hundred of the brothers at the same time, most of whom are still living, though some have fallen asleep. Then he appeared to James, then to all the Apostles, and last of all he appeared to me also, as to one abnormally born.

Paul says in effect, "If you do not believe me, you can ask them." When the disciples of Jesus proclaimed the resurrection, they did so as eyewitnesses, and they did so while people were still alive who had contact with the events about which they spoke. Today, even though we were not there to personally witness this event, we can know that it happened because Scripture has told the story, history supports it, and historians have written more on this subject than on any other historical event in history.

Professor Thomas Arnold, author of the three-volume "History of Rome," and an appointee to the chair of modern history at Oxford University, writes: "I know of no one fact in the history of mankind which is proved by better and fuller evidence of every sort, to the understanding of a fair inquirer, than the great sign which God had given us that Christ died and rose again from the dead."[2]

The personal transformation of the disciples speaks louder than the written evidence as to the power of the resurrection of Christ. Since the resurrection of Christ, all who believe that Christ did in fact die and rise again, are given the gift of the Holy Spirit, the invisible God, Himself living in us. We now are free to live in union with God. Imagine that, having a deep personal relationship that will never end with the God who created the world and all that is in it.

I used to think that God couldn't possibly have the time to have a personal relationship with all people. The truth is that He does, because we worship a Big God. As a result, our lives can and should be transformed just like those of the disciples. They were changed into courageous men who later died as martyrs. Not one of them ever denied the Lord or recanted his belief that Christ had indeed risen. This is unparalleled in history.

We, too, because of the death and resurrection of Christ, can now have the courage to live in this broken world with much love, hope, purpose and passion. God not only had a plan for Himself as Savior of the world, but for each of us.

Jeremiah 29:11-14 "For I know the plans I have for you," declares the Lord, "plans to prosper you and not to harm you, plans to give you hope and a future. Then you will call upon me and come and pray to me, and I will listen to you. You will seek me and find me when you seek me with all your heart. I will be found by you," declares the Lord, "and will bring you back from captivity."

By reading the whole story of the resurrection, there should be no doubt in your mind that God loves you, and proved it to you through the whole experience of the cross. If He can love those who whipped Him, drove nails into His flesh, spit and yelled obscenities at Him, then, my friend, He can and does love you right where you are at this moment. He told you He loved you and then proved it by dying on the cross for you. With the Holy Spirit living in you, you, too, can love the unlovable and forgive the unforgivable. You are now free to live out the life that God originally intended for you to live.

The truth of the death and resurrection of Christ will hold us secure in the very worst storms of life. Life circumstances often cause us to be disappointed, discouraged and detached from others. Knowing that Jesus is alive and that He is our hope is all that we will ever need. To know that He loves and cares for us enough to endure the cross must serve as a comfort to our souls.

:: **What difference does it make to me that Christ died for my sins?**
Matt's Story. The last time we saw Matt, he was being arrested by the police and taken to jail, and then was sent to a rehab center in Arizona. Things did not look good for Matt.

It was in this rehab center where the hardest, most painful (both emotionally and physically) days of my life occurred. On the third day of my stay in rehab, I was lying on the floor crying, because I was in so much pain. It was at this moment that I caught this vision of God telling me that He was not punishing me, nor was He judging me. He told me that He was there with open arms to go through this difficult time with me. From that moment on, I handed my life over to Christ, realizing His love for me and, since then, my life has never been the same.

I haven't touched drugs or alcohol since that time, over seven years ago. I chose not to have a girlfriend/relationship until I met the woman I wanted to marry. Since then, I have met and married my wife, Brittney. I went back to college, graduated with a 3.95 and got an accounting degree. I have a great job.

When times get hard for me, I have learned not to turn to myself, but I have learned to turn to God. This has been the most amazing change in my life.

I had a revelation a few years ago. I was in lifting weights, heavy weights, by myself. For those of you that lift weights, this was not a good idea. I was lifting a very large amount of weights and on the last rep, I couldn't get the bar up. I pinned myself with 225 pounds of weight on my chest. I started to panic, thinking I was going to die, but all of a sudden this guy comes in and picks the weight up off of my chest. Every time I see that guy, I acknowledge him for taking the weight off my chest. This is a perfect analogy for our Christian walk. We have this sin bearing down on our chest and we are suffocated by it. We know we can't handle it on our own, so we need to turn to someone else to help us. We, as Christians, rely on Christ, our Savior, to come running in and pick up the weight of our sins. Not only did He pick up that weight for us, but He had to die in order to get that weight off of our chest.

How much more should we be thinking everyday about what Christ has done for us? Once we can grasp, in our minds, the greatness of what He has done for us, then everything else in our life will just fall in line.

Because we believe in the death and resurrection of Christ, we know that when we die, we, like Jesus, will live again. Not because we have done anything on our own, but because of what Christ did for us on the cross. He died for the sins of the world, meaning that we do not have to suffer the consequences for our sin. John 3:1 "For God so loved the world that He gave His only Son, that whosoever believes in Him, shall not perish but will have everlasting life." That is our hope: that when a believer in Christ dies, God promises that that person will live forever with Him in heaven!

Either Jesus did or did not rise from the dead. It is your choice to accept or not accept this as being true. Based on all of the evidence, I found it takes much more faith not to believe than it does to believe. If it is true that Jesus did rise from the dead, we have the answers to the most profound questions about life that we could ask: "Why is there such a mess in the world? Is there hope? What is my purpose in life? What happens when I die?"

A few years ago, my mother became gravely ill. I had the privilege of spending much time with her throughout her dying process. She would talk about how she was anxious to see my dad, my brother, Stephen and others who had died. She spoke often of her love for Jesus and how she yearned to see Him. She had no fear of death, but the dying process was difficult for all of us. I was in constant communication with my children, updating them on their Gram's condition.

Mark, my son, knew how stressed I was in watching her suffer. He wrote to me the following note: "I thought I would let you know how I picture Gram at this moment in time. It helps me and may help you. I'm sure you have thought about all of this, but I thought I would share this with you. I have become more and more aware of the battles that are beyond our human understanding:

things that we can't see and those things that go way beyond what we feel, and what we know to be true in this world. You see your mother, sick and frail, lying in a bed alone, no longer the strong, full of life woman that you have known all your life. I see Gram lying in bed, surrounded by more angels than any bed could possibly hold, filling her with peace that you and I could never imagine or experience in our wildest dreams. They are holding her hands and stroking her forehead. She can see Granddad and Stephen. She can feel what it is like to be with them again. This is what she wants. She is not scared … you are. So take care of her, grieve for her, and be sad. It's OK. But next time you are in her room, take a close look … things may not be as they appear." *

On the last day of her life on this earth, I went in to see my mother. After talking to her hospice nurse, I knew that time was very short. As I went into her room, I found her lying in her bed and talking about this big party that she was going to attend. She described the flowers that were "out of this world," the food that was on the table, the children that were running around and the beautiful music that was playing. She began to sing along with what she was hearing. She was so happy and excited about the big event that she was about to attend. I thought of Mark's note to me and I did take a closer look. I didn't see any angels, but I had the feeling my mother might have been witnessing the last minute preparations for her homecoming party. The sadness of what was about to happen was overshadowed by her joy. Soon the time came to say goodbye with the understanding that it was not forever. I know that I will see her again in heaven. Why? Because He lives!

Her death brought many tears, coupled with countless wonderful stories about her life and experiences that we all had shared with her. The pain of her death was tempered, because without a doubt, I know where she is today and for that, I can celebrate with her. Dance on, Mom!

* These words were written to me by the same son I mentioned in the previous chapter, who struggled with doubt. Even in his doubt, he continued to seek God. Fifteen years later, Mark was able to encourage and comfort his mother which is a true testament of God's faithfulness to those who seek Him. :: :: ::

:: What God?

TOOLS OF THE TRADE ::

chapter 5

most all of us know someone who claims to be an

atheist. An atheist is a person who denies that there is a God. Some are just more verbal about it than others. Diane, a close friend of mine, does more for others than anyone else I know. If someone wants something done well, they will call Diane. She is kind, loving and would give you all she had, if necessary. If God had a heavenly scale where He weighed good deeds against bad deeds, she would be first in line. Diane believes in her own idea of God, but openly rejects the person of Jesus Christ. She so typically reflects the Postmodern thinker, in that she believes that her god is good for her, and that if I want to believe in Jesus Christ of Scripture that is fine also; just don't try to tell her what she should believe. To her, there are no absolutes, especially when it comes to God. "He is whatever you want him to be," she would say to me. Finally, one day I asked her to have lunch with me, because there was something that I wanted to share with her.

An atheist is someone who denies that there is a God, while an agnostic does not believe in God, but will acknowledge the possibility of one. My goal in this conversation was to take her from a full rejection of God to at least consider that there may be a God out there that she has yet to meet. In other words, I wanted to take her from an atheist point of view to that of an agnostic. Sometimes as Christians speaking to non-Christians, we are convinced that we have to lead someone into a relationship with Christ. Remember that surrendering one's life to Christ is usually a culmination of life experiences and truth being revealed over time. In many cases, gentle conversations that encourage one to merely consider their faith and compare it to the truth you have to offer are key in that process.

We met and in the course of our conversation, we talked about a mutual friend's mother who had just died. "Diane, if you were to die today, are you certain that you would go to heaven?" I asked.

"I have no clue what that is," she said, "but if it is a place where good people go, then I think that I qualify. I have led a good life and haven't tried to hurt anyone."

"Would you like to know for sure?" I inquired.

"Not if it involves Jesus. I do not want to be a Jesus freak. Besides, I don't believe in Him anyway," she responded. I must say, I was a bit taken back with her response.

Remembering something that I had read from C.S. Lewis, I took my napkin and a pen, and drew a circle. "This circle represents all of the knowledge, truth and experiences from all times. How much of this have you experienced?" I asked.

She looked a bit puzzled, as I gave her the pen and asked her to shade in what she had experienced. She thought for a minute and said, "Sadly, not much," and she placed a very small dot in the circle on the napkin.

I replied, "I'm not saying that it happened, but do you think, that outside of your own human experiences, that there could have been a time when God sent His Son to earth to live and die for all the sins of mankind, and then rise again to life? Could it be that He did it for you and all He is asking of you is to believe in Him? Might there be, I'm not saying that it is true, but might there be the possibility that if you chose to believe, you could be certain that when you die you would go to heaven and live with God forever?" I then drew a cross in the circle close to, but not intersecting the dot that she had made.

She just sat and stared at the napkin. I was a bit worried that I had said too much, but I didn't want to leave anything out! "I guess if you put it that way, there could be," she said.

"How do you think that your life might be different if all of what I said were true?" I continued.

"I guess I wouldn't worry so much about dying. I think that I would be happier," Diane replied.

"Would you be willing to meet with me once a week for an hour and study with me to see if what I am suggesting is true?"

I was shocked that she jumped at the chance to meet. We had a deal.

We are still meeting and as of this moment, she has not made a commitment to Christ, but she is hanging in there and asking lots of questions and reading her new Bible. I trust God to continue to bring her to Him.

Why is it so important that we know the foundational truths of the Christian faith? Because of all the Dianes in the world who need someone to sit with them, when the time is right, and share with them the love of God, and the possibility of knowing Him personally. The idea here is to have the atheist see that there are occurrences, perhaps even truths, that exist beyond his/her own personal experience. This opens the door to plant a seed of doubt in their mind that might cause the person to question his/her godless faith, and open a dialogue with them about a personal God that loves them and has a plan and purpose for their life.

As a long time nonbeliever, there was nothing more obnoxious than to have someone approaching total strangers and asking them to receive Jesus, as if it were some kind of contest. Some of my friends would pray with these people just to get them to leave. Bringing someone to Christ is a very serious thing, and most of the time, involves a commitment of time to meet with and teach the foundations of the faith to your friend. The following is a strategy that I use personally and teach as we interface with those God has given us.

:: The strategy is the five "L"s

Learn the truths of the Christian faith.

Live them out in your life in everything that you do. No one that is truly a Christian can choose the times to "act" like a believer, they simply must BE one. In essence, they must live out the Christian worldview.

Listen to others. Be quick to listen and slow to speak. Learn their story, how they think, and the "God" experiences that they have had in their life.

Love them right where they are right now. Don't ask them to change; be like Jesus and love them, sin and all. Consider them to be a friend.

Lead them, when God urges you, to tell them the truth of the good news of Jesus Christ. Speak to them in their language, using their life experiences to explain the gospel. They want to know how the Christian life might work in their life, not yours. Stay away from teaching them what they have or have not to do. Leave that up to God as He will, through the Holy Spirit, direct the new believer through the Scriptures.

Making ourselves available to be used by God takes lots of our time, but compared to the joy of being a part of bringing someone into a personal relationship with Christ, that makes it all worth it! Kristin is a former student and has a gift of being slow to speak, but quick to listen and to love. She also has the gift of adventure, as you will see as you read her story.

Kristin's Story. I met Martin the summer of '05 at a youth hostel in Northern Scotland. I recall clearly days marked by a heavy fog and sheets of rain, necessitating many cups of hot tea to be sipped by the fire, along with other hostel guests. My friend, Kim, and I had traveled that summer to Europe to be short-term vagabonds. Along with thousands of other kids our age, we wanted to journey to the other side of the world and taste other cultures, meet interesting people and hear stories of how their lives were unique from our own.

Martin was a painter and musician, originally from London proper. He'd been homeless since he was a teenager, and after working his way through a vocational art school, he had traveled all over Europe, painting and living in youth hostels, like the one we were staying in. I remember him being incredibly kind and personable. As we sat by the fire with him, he unfolded details of his life journey with us and we, in return, shared our stories with him.

As the days transpired, a couple of other weary travelers joined our conversations: a boy from South Africa and one from Israel. You can only imagine how interesting our dialogue became! We quickly learned the value of listening, and asking our fellow travelers to divulge their opinions and experiences with us. How rich we become when we listen! We conversed about everything imaginable, for, because of the weather, we had nowhere else to go!

Toward the end of our stay, after we had gone in conversational circles around politics, education, religion, sex, money, ending poverty and digressing to our favorite travel stories, we entered into one of the liveliest, most insightful discussions about Jesus Christ that I've ever had. The life experiences, the stories, represented in these friends were vast, and as we shared of our experiences of the Divine, God showed up and changed lives.

Most of all, He began to change a portion of my life. I realized as we all sat scattered around couches, as the rain poured down outside, that being able to discuss, question and dialogue about truth is one of the most essential aspects of our being. As I am encouraged to delve deeper into my faith through dialogue with others, my journey becomes all the more strengthened. Space to honestly pursue God with a community of others naturally develops faith. Listening. Asking. Questioning. Learning. All these things produced in me a fuller, more personal and authentic relationship with God.

I began walking with Jesus (or running to catch up with Him!) in November of 1998. Despite my commitment and my passion for the Gospel, I had endless questions. You see, I came to know God was real because of a relationship He started with me, and that only further produced a deeper hunger to answer questions I had about who He is. Up until the spring of 2000, when I began attending Anchorsaway classes, I had no one who was willing or able to begin walking with me through this process.

We don't have much space for this type of dialogue in our culture, especially in our Christian culture. A myriad of voices, both positive and negative, inform us that there is a specific way to do things, yet these voices are often very different from one another! Even the Christian ones! With all these voices speaking, where do we have the opportunity to discern truth freely and authentically? As a young Christian, I knew Jesus intimately, but I longed to know more about Him. Where was I to find a good environment to discover more about God, along with other Christ-followers?

By far, the biggest strength of Anchorsaway is the community of honest, authentic truth-seekers that, together, ask hard questions and determine to find the answers. We all have questions. And deep down, we all want answers. But who and how we choose to ask will determine how fruitful our findings will be. Anchorsaway is not a "safe" community. You won't find the stale pat answers that you might be used to. Everything that you hear will wake up your faith. Everything that you hear will jolt you into deeper communion with God. Because everything you hear is revolutionary. The Gospel is revolutionary. Since the very beginning, a relationship with God has meant radical life transformation. It changes lives. Are you ready for yours to be changed, too?

I again stand in awe of our Sovereign Almighty God, who not only wants to have a relationship with us, but with our friends, as well! The remarkable thing is that He wants to use you and me, as imperfect as we are, in the process! I encourage you to use these tools of the trade, not only with paper and pen, but in words and deeds, as you try to encourage your friend to consider something about God that might be new to them. Prepare to be amazed! :: :: ::

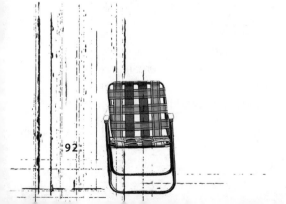

IT'S ALL IN THE NAME ::

chapter 6

have you ever noticed how easy it is to talk about God, but

to talk openly about Jesus is taboo? If you are looking for a great way to ruin a discussion at work, in school or in a social gathering, just talk about Jesus. Why is that so? Postmodernly speaking, might it be that "god" is a generic term to mean whatever you want it to mean?

Jesus. Is there something about that name? The very mention of "Jesus" oftentimes narrows the field as people become very emotional about what they think concerning this man who is called The Savior. In Mark 8:27 Jesus questioned his disciples, asking them, "Who do people say I am?" The answers they gave Him were as varied as they are today. Our world is saturated with a variety of ideas about Jesus. There are some, as taught by Mormon doctrine, that embrace the radical notion that Jesus was the brother of Lucifer, while others believe He was just a prophet. Many say He was a great moral teacher and philosopher, "a wonderful wise man, nothing more."[1] Still others suggest He was the greatest human being to ever walk the earth.

Who is this Jesus? Can God be God without Jesus?

If you have read the previous chapters and perhaps have done your own research, I assume that you would agree with the research that the Bible is reliable and that Christ did rise from the dead. All of this points to the truth that Jesus Christ is God. Man could not defeat death; only God could do that!

Is Jesus Christ God? This is the fundamental question that each of us must answer if we are to ever know true salvation. The Christian worldview, in contrast to all other religions and belief systems, is built on the conviction that Jesus Christ was more than merely a good teacher, a prophet or wise sage. He is God incarnate, and His deity has an overwhelming impact on mankind.

A biblical understanding of the Trinity will settle the debate of the divinity of Jesus. It will also answer a multitude of questions that we have regarding cults and other religions. It will give us insight into the beauty of God we see in the perfect love relationship between the Father, the Son and the Holy Spirit.

What is the Trinity? According to Dr. James White, "The doctrine of the Trinity is simply that there is one eternal being of God – indivisible and infinite. This one being of God is shared by three co-equal, co-eternal persons: the Father, the Son and the Spirit.

"The three biblical doctrines that flow directly into the river that is the Trinity are as follows:

1. There is one and only one God, eternal, immutable.

2. There are three eternal Persons described in Scripture – the Father, the Son and the Spirit. These Persons are never identified as one in the same – that is, they are clearly differentiated as Persons. (The Father is not the Son, nor is He the Holy Spirit. The Son is not the Father, nor is He the Holy Spirit. The Holy Spirit is not the Son, nor the Father.)

3. The Father, the Son and the Spirit are identified as being fully deity – that is, the Bible teaches the Deity of Christ and the Deity of the Holy Spirit."

The word "Trinity" is not used directly in Scripture, but the concept of the Trinity is found throughout. A few of those references follow: Creation (Genesis 1:1-2; John 1:1-3), Christ's birth (Luke 1:30-35), and The Great Commission (Matthew 28:19).

The significance of the Trinity for us is this: One of the foundational beliefs of Christianity, which sets it apart from religious cults and all other belief systems, is the conviction that Jesus is truly God. In no way does Jesus play a supporting role to the Father and the Holy Spirit. He is fully God just as they are, an equal member of the Trinity. If someone says to you, "I believe in God, but not Jesus," you would know immediately that the person with whom you are speaking is, at best, confused. God is not God without Jesus. God is not God without the Father. And God is not God without the Holy Spirit. God is one being with three persons.

Is the Bible consistent internally in its portrayal of Christ's deity in the Old and New Testaments? This may surprise you, but Jesus is called:

Creator (John 1:3, Colossians 1:15-17, Hebrews 1:10)

Lord of Lords and King of Kings (Revelation 17:14, 19:16, 1 Timothy 6:14-16)

Savior (Acts 2:21, 4:12, Romans 10:9)

Rock (1 Corinthians 10:4, Isaiah 8:14)

The First and the Last (Revelation 1:17, 2:8, 22:13)

Judge (2 Timothy 4:1, 2 Corinthians 5:10, Romans 14:10)

I AM (John 8:24, 58; 13:19, 18:5).

So many of these terms are often thought to be reserved for God (Yahweh), but are also manifested in Christ, Himself. What does all of this mean? Jesus is God!

Because Jesus died for the sins of the world, He is the Savior. Why Jesus instead of some other person or animal used as a sacrifice for our sins? The answer is because Jesus is Holy and without sin and, therefore, He alone qualified to be the Redeemer for all of humanity. God required a perfect sacrifice to satisfy a perfect, sinless God. Anything less than perfect did not satisfy a Holy God, therefore God, the Son, had to come from heaven and take on the sin of all the world, and then pay the ultimate penalty for sin (Romans 6:23), which is death. That is why Jesus had to die on the cross, so that the penalty of your sins, death, would be paid in full, making you righteous in the eyes of a Holy God. Not because of what you did, but because of what God did for you! Yes, you! Your relationship is made right with God when you accept and believe that He died for you.

The Christian writer C.S. Lewis, explains the significance of Christ's claims to deity: "… Among these Jews there suddenly turns up a man who goes about talking as if He was God. He claims to forgive sins. He says He has always existed. He says He is coming to judge the world at the end of time. Now let us get this clear. Among Pantheists, like the Indians, anyone might say that he was a part of God, or one with God: there would be nothing very odd about it. But this man, since He was a Jew, could not mean that kind of God. God in their language meant the Being outside the world Who had made it and was infinitely different from anything else. And when you have grasped that, you will see that what this man said was, quite simply, the most shocking thing that has ever been uttered by human lips … I am trying here to prevent anyone saying the really foolish thing that people often say about Him: 'I'm ready to accept Jesus as a great moral teacher, but I don't accept His claim to be God.' That is the one thing we must not say. A man who was merely a man and said the sort of things Jesus said, would not be a great moral teacher. He would either be a lunatic—on a level with the man who says he is a poached egg—or else he should be the Devil of Hell. You must make your choice. Either this man was, and is, the Son of God: or else a madman or something worse. You can shut Him up for a fool, you can spit at Him and kill Him as a demon; or you can fall at His feet and call Him Lord and God. But let us not come with any patronizing nonsense about His being a great human teacher. He has not left that open to us. He did not intend to."[2]

To truly know Jesus Christ is to recognize that He is nothing less than God. The divinity of Jesus Christ is what sets Christianity apart from all other religions, and we can stand confidently on the claims to His deity.

The fact that Jesus was more than just a man, that He was truly God, should give us a sobering appreciation for the sacrifices He willingly made so that we might be saved. Our salvation means that God first comes to us; man does not have to invent a way to find Him first. Nor do we have to earn our way to heaven; salvation is God's gift of grace to those who are willing to accept it. And when we do accept Jesus as our Lord and Savior, we are promised by God to live with Him forever!

The rest but not the end of Brett's Story. In the spring of 2004, Brett was called to go to Afghanistan with the Army National Guard's 76th Infantry Brigade in Operation Enduring Freedom. He left in the summer and returned for a two-week visit over Thanksgiving of that year. On March 26, 2005, the vehicle that Brett and three fellow soldiers were riding in drove over a landmine. They were all killed instantly.

Many asked the question that you are probably asking yourself: Why, God? He loved you and was there on an "operation enduring freedom in Christ" mission of his own. He was one of the most outstanding Christian men that many of us have known, and you called him home. From my perspective here on earth it makes little sense. From Your perspective, Lord, You knew that Brett wanted his life to count for You, and wanted You to use him to bring others to Christ.

The impact of Brett's life was made evident upon his death, as hundreds of people, young and old, attended the memorial service held in Bloomington, Indiana, following his death. Each of his family members, his fiancée, and best friends stood before the crowd and testified of Brett's love and faith. Others were invited to come up and share their memories of Brett, and the impact that he made on their lives. The story-telling lasted well into the night.

On his grave stone is carved, "Present with the Lord Jesus. Loved well, well loved."

It is not wishful thinking that Brett is present with the Lord Jesus. It is the truth. The Scriptures declare it and the Scriptures are the Word of God. We also know that Jesus, being God, was the perfect and only sacrifice for the sins of all mankind. Brett believed, received, and is now going to be a part of the greeting party when his friends, who also believe, will depart from this earth and join him in heaven.

Who is this God that would do such a thing for us? He is the Creator of the universe whose love for us is beyond measure. Jesus offered Himself as a living sacrifice, because He desperately wants to be in a personal relationship with us. We need only to accept this free gift from God. Jesus has told us, "Here I am! I stand at the door and knock. If anyone hears my voice and opens the door, I will come in …" (Revelation 3:20).

My friend, I must ask you, have you accepted Christ's gift of salvation? Jesus does not stand far off. He is right here, waiting for you to respond to Him. Once you take the necessary step to know the God of the universe, your life will never be the same again! :: :: ::

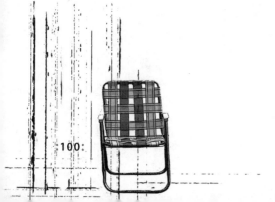

100

AM I? ::

chapter 7

:: **What God?**

when applying to college, I had to fill out a student

profile questionnaire asking, among other things, what religion I practiced. With little thought, I checked Christian because I knew I wasn't a Jew or a Hindu. During the fall of my freshman year, it was reported in an article in the school paper that the vast majority of the freshmen on campus were Christians. In retrospect, I find that interesting. While at school I looked for a Christian to answer some questions I had concerning Christianity, but I never found one who could do so. Apparently my colleagues had filled out that student profile form the same way I did! I have a feeling that many think that being born in America, attending church on Christmas Eve or on Easter, would put them in the Christian arena. Interestingly, today's statistics support such misconceptions. According to pollster George Barna, 85 percent of people in the United States claim to be Christians.[1] The Barna Group stats also show that only 9 percent of born again Christians believe in moral absolutes, and only 4 percent are genuinely committed to living out the Christian worldview.[2] These numbers do not add up. Should there not be close to 85 percent of born again Christians believing in moral absolutes, and similar numbers who are living out the Christian worldview? Could it be that people do not have a clear understanding of what it truly means to be a genuine Christian?

Opinion polls aside, what does it mean to be an authentic Christian? A person does not become a Christian just by coming forward at an altar call or repeating a prayer. God looks at the heart of a person and never has been impressed with idle words.

1 Samuel 16:7 The LORD does not look at the things man looks at. Man looks at the outward appearance, but the LORD looks at the heart."

If the words are not reflecting the attitude of the heart, then they fall on deaf ears. Becoming a Christian, a follower of Christ, is a gift from God by way of the cross, to all who choose to believe that Jesus Christ is God and the only Savior of the world.

John 3:16 For God so loved the world that he gave his one and only Son, that whoever believes in him shall not perish but have eternal life.

The Greek word for believe, *pisteuo*, means "to be persuaded of." Therefore, to believe in Jesus is "to place confidence in, to trust"[3] in Him. It is more than a mere credence; it requires a commitment to live it out, which follows one's declaration of faith.

Let me put it this way. The concept of a genuine belief in Christ might be understood in what I call the Potawatomi Principle. When I was in third grade, our class studied about the Potawatomi Indians who lived in Michigan. I learned about wigwams and the lodges that they lived in and about the food they ate. I loved looking at pictures of guys with Mohawks and girls with the beaded shirts. There was historical documented evidence, as well as artifacts, that proved beyond a shadow of a doubt that the Potawatomi Indians existed and, as a matter of fact, still do today. I genuinely believed the Potawatomi existed, but knowing that fact did not, and does not, in the least bit, influence how I think, or how I choose to spend my time and money and energy.

Knowing and believing in Christ is quite another story. I place my total trust in Christ, and am committed to live out my faith in my daily life. Because I believe (pisteuo), the Spirit of God lives in me and I can choose to let my life reflect Christ in all I do. It is my desire, and hopefully, the desire of all who believe, to love God with all of my heart, soul and strength. (Deuteronomy 6:5) Am I always successful in this endeavor? Absolutely not. But regardless of my failure, it is still my heart's desire.

:: Not by good works

Unlike all cults and other religions, salvation has nothing to do with works. By works, I mean earning your way to heaven by something you do, something you have earned, or by being a certain someone. Ephesians 2:8-9 says, "For it is by grace you have been saved, through faith—and this not from yourselves, it is the gift of God—not by works, so that no one can boast." The good works of a true believer come as a result of the gratefulness for all that God has done and for all that He is. It is love, not duty, which motivates how we are to live.

Jesus established the criteria for living our lives. His disciples were called to "Come, follow me ..." (Matthew 4:19a). According to speaker and writer, Rob Bell, the invitation to come and follow Jesus was an invitation to "come with me and become like me." To know what it means to be a follower of Christ, we must know and obey Christ in a way that we might become more like Him.

As we have found in previous chapters, Jesus is the Messiah, the Lord and Savior of the world. Christ, the God-man, gave up His position in heaven and came to earth to teach, love, disciple, heal, fellowship, call people to Himself, suffer and die for the sins of the world (Philippians 2).

> **"Jesus our Savior** left heaven above,
> Coming to earth as a Servant with love;
> Laying aside all His glory, He came,
> Bringing salvation through faith in His name.[4]
> *– Hess*

An authentic faith reflects a belief in, and a commitment to, Christ that is built on love and obedience, those qualities that embodied His life on earth. As Christ was salt and light to the world, we, too, are called to imitate Christ (Matthew 5:13-16). The way we live should reflect the presence of the Holy Spirit, and bear witness to the genuineness of our faith and our loyalty to Jesus Christ (Galatians 5:22-25; 1 John 2:6). God's will for our lives is to walk with Him through the power of the Holy Spirit. In essence, we are called by God to live out the Christian worldview!

Kelly's story. Ahh … college! Everyone steps onto campus with a different mix of emotions—for some it is a long-awaited breath of fresh air, for others a terrifying step of independence. The time between being dropped off at the dorms of a secular state university as a freshman, and the graduation ceremony as a senior, was filled with incredible memories, challenging times and a lot of growth for me, personally and spiritually.

If asked to pass on one bit of advice, it would be the following verses: Psalm 37:4-7 "Delight yourself in the Lord and he will give you the desires of your heart. Commit your way to the Lord; trust in him and he will do this: He will make your righteousness shine like the dawn, the justice of your cause like the noonday sun."

:: "Delight yourself in the Lord…"

I was introduced to God early on and grew up with an appreciation and respect for authentic faith in Jesus. I accepted Christ as my Savior at a young age. Despite periods of my life when I was simply going through the motions, by the time I was leaving for college, I had developed a personal relationship with God that I was excited and passionate about. It was not a faith that was there to please my parents or one that had been forced upon me, it was my own and I was reliant upon it as my source of confidence, purpose and joy!

:: "...and he will give you the desires of your heart."

College can be a selfish time as you are consumed with your own schedule, own plans and own goals. I had my mind set on what I wanted in college: good grades, a spot on the varsity tennis team, four years of great memories with friends and fun stories. There is a difference between having your own selfish desires and trying to manipulate them to please God, versus seeking God's desires for your life and freely acting upon them. I had a picture of what I wanted out of the upcoming four years, but had to learn patience; understanding God blesses in doses. I learned to live day-by-day, not looking too far ahead and missing what was right around me.

:: "Commit your way to the Lord; trust in him..."

I was determined to make a difference and live a life that was a good witness for Christ. I wasn't sure how. I struggled between this and wanting to meet friends, be accepted and be a part of everything from the beginning. I did not want to push people away or be seen as "close-minded" or "judgmental" if I was outspoken about my faith or decided not to drink. Would anyone even notice or ask why? Was it worth it? What was I missing out on? Looking back, how I chose to live out my college years by being faithful to God's call was a great decision. God did not call me into a holy huddle, but rather to love and develop friendships with many different kinds of people; I did not shy away from friendships or relationships with anyone. I did not separate myself from the parties or the bars—I jumped in, had a blast, but just made a commitment not to drink. People noticed. People don't want to meet martyrs who sulk about restrictions they have placed on their lives, they want to meet people who love life and love people. They will see that you are driven by a stronger passion and a genuine love for life; then they will ask, and you will be ready to answer. The goal is to have people take a second look and question why you are different. I thrived on that—on being different, so they could see that I had a joy and a peace that went deeper than close friends, good grades and athletics. All gifts given to me by our God through "the riches of God's grace that he lavished on us with all wisdom and understanding (Ephesians 1:7, 8; 1 John 3:1).

:: "He will make your righteousness shine like the dawn, the justice of your cause like the noonday sun."

You may not see it at the time ... I didn't, but you are making an impact when you choose to be faithful to God's call on your life. I found an email from a friend in college with whom I studied abroad: "This last semester, I have been going through lots of changes and I have you to thank for part of that. On July 4, 1996, I sat in a café in Paris with a wonderful girl and we talked about everything—herself, her morality, her beliefs. All I could say was, 'I used to think that.' 'I used to be that way.' I have thought about that a lot this semester. You made me realize that I was in a phase where I wasn't myself. This semester I am going back to my ways and adding more 'good' things to my life. I'm not drinking to get drunk, and most importantly, I am going to church. Thanks."

There are things I would have done differently in my life, but as for my convictions and decision to live out my faith, I would never change that. At times I stumble and struggle, but am never out of the grasp of God. I believe the most impacting thing a Christian can do is to be real and live out an authentic life in Christ. Please do not separate yourself from others who do not share the same beliefs or convictions—but rather, respect the differences. Live a life that is sincere, and joy-filled ... place yourself in people's lives ... make yourself vulnerable by opening up and being honest ... be ready for people to question what it is about you that makes you tick ... and then be ready to answer. What an incredible privilege it is to be a child of God!

I thank God for people like Kelly who set their minds on God's will, instead of their own. On what did Kelly miss out? Not much. Did some people think that she was weird for not drinking? No doubt about it. Did she have times of loneliness? Absolutely. Is there a cost to following Christ? Yes. To think that we, as Christians, will escape all controversy, pain and suffering is unrealistic. We can take comfort in knowing that our Lord, who calls us to imitate Him, experienced all of those things, Himself!

:: Why should we follow Him?

So why should I follow Him if I am going to experience all of those difficult things? Whether or not you follow Christ, you will experience suffering and trials. That is part of living in this world. The majority of suffering that we all face comes about in a multitude of ways, many of which are the consequences of bad life decisions. The Christians who choose to follow Christ are spared from many of the consequences of making poor life choices. Think about it, someone living as a committed Christian will not have to worry about making a fool out of themselves for drinking too much, or experience the devastating effects of alcohol, because they commit to living by the Holy Spirit (Ephesians

5:18). They will not ever have to worry about being pregnant outside of marriage or getting a venereal disease, or having to deal with the pain and guilt of an abortion.

Yes, there is one more thing: the believer never has to worry about where they are going to spend eternity. God promises that the believer will have life and will spend eternity in heaven with God and all others who have believed (1 John 5:12-13).

:: **Where do you stand?**

Up to this point in this book, you have read the proof, and now hopefully know, or are seriously considering, the reliability of the Bible, the death and resurrection of Christ, the deity of Christ and the truth as to God's identity. Knowing this is essential in building your faith in Jesus Christ. It does NOT, however, make you a Christian.

Consider four groups of people. There are those who are:

> **Saved by faith through Christ and know it.** (Those who believe that Jesus Christ is God and died for their sins and rose again. They have assurance that they are God's children.)
> **Saved by faith through Christ and do not know it.** (People who believe that Jesus Christ is God and died for their sins and rose again. They think that there must be something else that they must do or be in order to become one of His children. For others, they feel completely undeserving and cannot fathom being accepted into God's family.)
> **Not saved by faith through Christ and know it.** (This is for those who have heard the truth of Christ and knowingly reject it.)
> **Not saved by faith through Christ and do not know it.** (They think that they are Christians, but are not.)

This fourth group claims or thinks that they are Christians, but in reality are not, because they are ignorant regarding the commitment and statutes required by authentic faith. I believe that this is the group of evangelicals that the Barna Group said claim to be Christian (85%), but are not living out the Christian worldview. They would be identified as the worldview called Neo-Christianity. This is comprised of those who have made an intellectual acknowledgement of Jesus Christ, with no heart commitment, that is then followed by no life change. Matthew 7:16-20 says, "By their fruit you will recognize them. Do people pick grapes from thorn bushes, or figs from thistles? Likewise every good tree bears good fruit, but a bad tree bears bad fruit. A good tree cannot bear bad fruit, and a bad tree cannot bear good fruit. Every tree that does not bear good fruit is cut down and thrown into the fire. Thus, by their fruit you will recognize them." If you (or they) are not producing fruit (see Fruit of the Spirit from earlier), then it is good to ask if you are truly a Christ follower.

Many of these people have grown up in Christian homes and know the "Christian verbiage," but live a life reflective of the world and not that of Jesus Christ. They lack a genuine, committed faith and are generally caught up in their own self-indulgences. Many of these people are the ones that others call hypocrites, because they will talk a good Christian game, but refuse to live one.

> **Tyler's Story.** The most important thing for me in college was finding friends with similar Christian beliefs as me. For me, developing Christian relationships is the most important ingredient for remaining on a path directed towards Christ. Let me rephrase that, real authentic Christian relationships are the most important factor for remaining true to my commitment to Christ. Finding the real Christians presented to me a huge challenge.
>
> I attended a private school in Georgia where the majority of students claimed to be Christian. Their idea of being a Christian and mine were miles apart. I never enjoyed knowing people who were eager to do something with one group of friends, but scared to do it around others. The vast majority of those who I knew that claimed to be Christians were adamant about going to church on Sundays, and had great manners when being around girls or their parents, but outside of that, anything, and I mean anything, was permissible. This kind of behavior never changed for the years that I attended the school.
>
> I loved the school and am glad that I chose it, but I found it disheartening to see the lack of true commitment to their faith in Christ. All that seems like an exercise in futility, because God knows exactly where you stand on each and every issue; He is the only one who matters anyway. I did find one great Christian friend who lived out his faith and was a great encouragement to me. That made it easier for me not to let other people's opinions about me affect me.

If this strikes a chord with your spirit, know that God is a God of second chances. There is nothing that you have done for which God will not forgive. Sadly enough, I believe that a great number of traditional church-goers fall into this category. I am encouraging, no, I am pleading with you to go before your

God and ask Him to examine your heart and reveal to you where you are in relation to His saving grace. This is between you and God alone. No other person can do anything about this issue. It is up to you. Take courage, be honest and repentant before God, and begin to live the life that God has planned for you, a life that will give you great peace and joy!

As an encouragement, allow me share with you a story about Roy "Wrong Way" Riegles and the 1929 Rose Bowl game between Georgia Tech and California. After scooping up a fumble by the other team just before halftime, California's Roy Riegles became disoriented and ran toward his own goal. As he was about to run the ball into the end zone, he was tackled by his own teammate at the one-yard line. During the halftime of that infamous Rose Bowl game, Riegles was understandably devastated by what he had done, and sat over in the corner with his head under a towel. Before heading back out on to the field, the coach announced that he was going to keep the original starters in the game. As the rest of the team headed out of the locker room, Roy didn't move, protesting to the coach that he had ruined the game and was too embarrassed to go back in. His coach responded, "Riegles, the game is only half over."[5]

Not only do we worship a God of second chances, but we also love our God for all He is and for all He has done for us as believers. God truly does lavish us with gifts. Check these out. The following "I am" statements provide asurances for all believers.[6]

> **I am** a child of God (John 1:12).
> **I am** Christ's friend (John 15:15).
> **I am** chosen and appointed by Christ to bear His fruit (John 15:16).
> **I am** a son of God; God is spiritually my Father (Romans 8:14, 15; Galatians 3:26; 4:6).
> **I am** a joint heir with Christ, sharing His inheritance with Him (Romans 8:17).
> **I am** a temple, a dwelling place of God. His Spirit and His life dwell in me (1 Corinthians 3:16, 6:19).
> **I am** a new creation (2 Corinthians 5:17).
> **I am** an heir of God since I am a son of God (Galatians 4:6, 7).
> **I am** a saint (Ephesians 1:1; 1 Corinthians 1:2; Philippians 1:1; Colossians 1:2).
> **I am** a fellow citizen with the rest of God's family (Ephesians 2:19).
> **I am** righteous and holy (Ephesians 4:24).
> **I am** a citizen of heaven, seated in heaven right now (Philippians 3:20;

Ephesians 2:6).
I am an expression of the life of Christ because He is my life
(Colossians 3:4).
I am chosen of God, holy and dearly loved (Colossians 3:12;
1 Thessalonians 1:4).
I am a son of light and not of darkness (1 Thessalonians 5:5).
I am born of God, and the evil one—the Devil—cannot touch me
(1 John 5:18).
I am NOT the great "I am" (Exodus 3:14; John 3:28, 8:58), but by the grace
of God, I am what I am (1 Corinthians 15:10).[7]

Andy's Story (Matt's twin brother). By the time that I was a senior in
high school, I was going to church, going to youth group every now and
then, and going to events like Anchorsaway. I don't know if it was the fact
that I was just really good at playing the hiding game, or that no one in
my life really loved me enough to challenge me. Maybe it was that no
one in my life really loved the cross of Christ enough to challenge me in
the way that I was living. But, really, by the time I was a senior, I never
expected myself to be at that point; living a life so far away from God.

Long story short, it came down to the fact that I was all about one thing:
me. I was pretty much getting drunk every weekend, getting high when I
had a chance to, and doing all the other things that go along with that
lifestyle in high school. I do remember going to Anchorsaway. We'd meet
in the basement and I'd think to myself: "These people here have no clue
how darn crazy I am." I look back over that time and the way that I was
living—my parents were kind of getting mad at me, but I was pretty good
at the hiding game with them. All my friends in my life were doing
exactly the same thing as me, so none of them could step up to me and
challenge me: "Okay, you're claiming the name of Christ, but you're living
like this." We were all living the same way and there was no one in my
group to hold me accountable. When I look back on it, I wish I would
have been challenged in high school about playing this double game.

I want to tell you a story about a time when I was challenged. It was after
I graduated from high school. My parents wanted me to go to this
Christian camp about worldviews and I was not excited about it, but they
forced me to go. On our way to camp, my parents and I had a huge fight
about substances, and they didn't want to drive the five-hour trip to
come pick me up at the end of the week. So I got a call the last day:
"Andy, we're going to fly you home on a plane." I had to wait around with

all these people at the camp. While I was waiting, this guy spoke some of the most loving words to me that I had ever heard in my life. I remember them so clearly. He said, "Andy, I've been watching you all week, and can I ask you this: Are you really a Christian?" He flat out, stepped up to me and asked me that. That dude had a lot of guts and that was a very loving thing for him to do, even though I didn't think so at the time. In response, I pretty much told him: "Hey, back off, man. I'm going through a rough time right now." I was totally depressed. I was on medication. I pretty much told him I didn't want to hear it.

As I think back on that conversation, I wish he would have gone even a step further, even though I would have hated hearing it. I wish he would have said, "Andy, do you even care about the cross of Christ? Do you realize about what the cross means and how this is God who has loved you, who died for your sins? Here you are claiming His name and then spitting in His face by your lifestyle?" I was an enemy to the cross of Christ by the way that I was living. I wish I could have thought about it in those terms, but really my heart was probably too hard to hear it then. God had a lot of breaking to do in my life.

I ended up going out West for college, and God, by His grace, broke me through my addiction to alcohol and being totally depressed. He broke me and He gave me a vision to see everything that I was searching for. I had been searching for fulfillment in being a Division 1 basketball player, in girls, in a fraternity, in alcohol and all these substances. Even though I was searching for satisfaction in these things, I was absolutely miserable. So, why was I staying in it? It was absolute insanity.

Then there was God saying, "Turn to Me. Come back to Me. You'll never have to search like this again." So, at that point, during my sophomore year at college, I told God, "I'm done with the game. You are so gracious that You want to call me to Yourself and You shower me with grace after I've cursed You, not only with my lips, but I've cursed Christ and God with my life." So, I came back to God and experienced His grace.

I guess, with you all, my one challenge would be, to ask you lovingly—I wish I knew you one on one—are you really a Christian? Does the cross of Christ mean anything to you? And if it does, feast on it. Feast on it and let it consume you, and realize that the Savior has taken your sins and the punishment you deserve. It is absolutely incredible. The punishment that we deserve, He has taken for us. He says, "I know you're a loser. I know you're a rebel, but here's grace. Believe in Me."

Here is one thing that will help you: remember that Jesus Christ is the Savior of your polluted soul and He has given you a new heart. And if you are convinced of the cross of Christ and that He is your Savior that will keep you. Where are you with the Lord?

:: We must make a choice

Maybe it is time, right now, to stop playing whatever game you are playing and honestly consider where you are with Christ the Lord. If Christ is who He says He is, then the question is, "What are you going to do with Him?" He died so that He could have a relationship with you. He loves you regardless of whether or not you love Him. Inviting Him into your life is the first step and as you grow in your relationship with Him, so will your love for Him. As with any new relationship it takes time to know someone intimately, so it is with God. It does not mean that you have to love Him immediately; that will come in time as it does with any new relationship. All He is asking is that you believe that He died for all of your sins: past, present and future. He died and rose again, proving to you that He lives and you can, too, forever with Him. That, my friend, is the Good News of all time!

Others of you have been playing the "Christian" game, with one foot in heaven and the other foot in the world. In many ways, your behavior is no different from that of non-Christians. You are not a reflection of God, but rather, a reflection of the world. Christ says that you are either for Me or against Me. You cannot have both. It is either God or the world; He leaves that choice up to you. Now is the time to make things right.

God not only is calling those who have never had a relationship with Him, but He is also calling those of you who are Christians, but for whatever reason are burned out and have walked away from God. Ask for forgiveness and invite Him once again to be the Lord of your life. Now is the time. Today is the day of salvation!

God does know your heart. If you would like to say a prayer affirming to God what you believe, do so. If you are wondering what such a prayer looks like, you can pray one like this: Dear God, I believe that Jesus Christ died for my sins and that He rose again. I know that by believing this, I am promised eternal life, and that I can come to You from now on as Your child. Thank You for forgiving me and loving me just as I am. Make me into the person that You created me to be.

Continue to reveal Yourself to me and to teach me what it is I need to know. In Jesus' name I pray. Amen.

If you believe that Jesus is God to the point that you are going to rely upon and trust God with the big and little things of your life, then let me welcome you to the family of God. You probably won't feel anything, but please know that you are, because of your faith, one of His, forever! Tell someone that you made a commitment, and start to learn about your Lord by reading Scripture, and hopefully, find a Bible-believing church where you worship and join others as they strengthen their relationship with Christ. If you have made a commitment to Christ, I promise you that it is the best decision that you will ever make. :: :: ::

IN THE BEGINNING ::

chapter 8

:: **What God?**

some of my favorite memories growing up were hay rides I took with friends out in the country fields, on cold October evenings. I loved it when we would pause in the pitch black of night and marvel at the apparent closeness and brilliance of the moon and the stars. I was awed with, not only the beauty of it all, but with the order of the universe. What held them up there in place day after day, year after year? Could the heavens with the moon and the stars have happened by chance, or was there a designer? Is the Christian totally ignorant to think that God could have created all this? Maybe, but then again, maybe not!

The Bible says that God created the world by speaking it into existence. Because the biblical creation account is outside the contemplative boundaries of our natural mind, many non-believers as well as Christians throw it out as being nothing more than a fable. If we follow the next logical step with this kind of thinking, we will seriously doubt the reliability of the Scriptures. This is nothing new. Through the ages, man has believed that if he can't understand the hows or whys of God, then it must not be. One of the cruxes of man is that we want the ways of God to fit into our realm of reason, and when they do not, we often times discount truth.

I love the conversation found in Scripture between God and Job. God was trying to teach Job that He, God, had everything under control, and that Job was a man that God loved, but yet just a man.

Job 38:1-21 Then the LORD answered Job out of the storm. He said: "Who is this that darkens my counsel with words without knowledge? Brace yourself like a man; I will question you, and you shall answer me.

"Where were you when I laid the earth's foundation? Tell me, if you understand. Who marked off its dimensions? Surely you know! Who stretched a measuring line across it? On what were its footings set, or who laid its cornerstone—while the morning stars sang together and all the angels shouted for joy?

"Who shut up the sea behind doors when it burst forth from the womb, when I made the clouds its garment and wrapped it in thick darkness, when I fixed limits for it and set its doors and bars in place, when I said, 'This far you may come and no farther; here is where your proud waves halt?' Have you ever given orders to the morning, or shown the dawn its place, that it might take the earth by the edges and shake the wicked out of it? The earth takes shape like clay under a seal; its features stand out like those of a garment. The wicked are denied their light, and their upraised arm is broken.

"Have you journeyed to the springs of the sea or walked in the recesses of the deep? Have the gates of death been shown to you? Have you seen the gates of the shadow of death? Have you comprehended the vast expanses of the earth? Tell me, if you know all this.

"What is the way to the abode of light? And where does darkness reside? Can you take them to their places? Do you know the paths to their dwellings? Surely you know, for you were already born! You have lived so many years!"

How often do we all forget that we are but finite creatures with very few answers about life? God is the great I AM of eternity, who might just have a bigger picture as to what life is all about, especially when it comes to Creation!

Psalm 8:3-4 (In the words of the Psalmist) "When I consider your heavens, the work of your fingers, the moon and the stars, which you have set in place, what is man that you are mindful of him, the son of man that you care for him ..."

All this begs the question, "If God placed the heavens in the sky, what about you and me?" If God spoke and the world was, then could God have done the same for the human race? I just don't get what all the controversy is about, except of course, if one chooses to leave God, the Intelligent Designer, out of the picture. If that happens, the only explanation of the how things and people come into being is through evolution. Seems to me this is more of a religious issue than a scientific one. If you are a Neo-Christian and trying to mix a little God with the theory of an atheistic scientist, then you might say that God started it and then evolution took over. The Bible does not in any way support this theistic evolution theory. One thing needs to be cleared up right away: this is not an issue of science vs. the Bible. Science supports the biblical account of creation, as you will see later in this chapter. The issue is the truth of Scripture vs. the theory of evolution. Let's begin at the beginning, to see if some light can be shed on this controversial topic that has been vigorously debated over the centuries.

Have you ever wondered from where you came? Our response to this fundamental life question has very profound implications as to how we think and live out our lives. It affects our morals and value systems, as well as how we love, forgive and appreciate others. It directly influences our understanding of the reliability and truth of the Scriptures. Our answer to this question about the origin of life shapes each person's worldview.

:: **What do the Scriptures and science have to say about creation?**

Genesis 1:1 tells us, "In the beginning God created …." For the Christian, this is the foundation for our worldview. Conversely, the prevailing belief of many scientists is that life is the result of random, evolutionary processes over millions of years. "In the beginning was the Big Bang …" say the scientists, and from there we gradually emerged from what Chuck Colson calls the "primordial soup."[1] We have all heard the merits of evolution being preached in every aspect of our culture, especially in our science classes, and in the news or on TV specials. The endorsement of evolution has become so commonplace that it is rarely questioned or challenged.

Genesis 1:1-3 In the beginning God created the heavens and the earth. Now the earth was formless and empty, darkness was over the surface of the deep, and the Spirit of God was hovering over the waters. And God said, 'Let there be light,' and there was light.

With that phrase, "Let there be light," the creation process began. An interesting note on the Hebrew word for God: it is "Elohim" which is the plural form of a singular God. Many scholars believe that this refers to the triune God: God the Father, Son and the Holy Spirit. This makes perfect sense, because later in Genesis 1:26 God said, "Let us make man in our image, in our likeness, and let them rule over the fish of the sea and the birds of the air, over the livestock, over all the earth, and over all the creatures that move along the ground."

Job 12:7-10 But ask the animals, and they will teach you, or the birds of the air, and they will tell you; or speak to the earth, and it will teach you, or let the fish of the sea inform you. Which of all these does not know that the hand of the LORD has done this? In his hand is the life of every creature and the breath of all mankind.

God has put the responsibility of what we believe about creation on each one of us, because He has made it obvious to mankind. You don't have to be a scientist to see the creative genius of our Creator. Take the time to look closely at a flower, or a butterfly or a hummingbird or a new born baby. Not too long ago, my family and I were standing on a beach in Florida along with at least a hundred or so vacationers, who had gathered to watch the sun set. Kids were playing in the sand and adults were talking with one another. As the sun went down on the horizon, the surrounding clouds lit the sky with the most beautiful splashes of reds, purples, oranges and yellows that you could ever see. Then a child began to clap with uncontrollable joy, overcome with the beauty of God's creation. Soon others joined in and before you knew it, all those on the beach were applauding the incredible splendor of the moment!

Not only do we see the Intelligent Designer in the heavens and in the earth, but we see it in Scripture. Elohim, the Creator God, is found in the Old Testament and the New Testament, giving the credit for creation to the Father, Son and Holy Spirit.

Romans 1:19-20 ... since what may be known about God is plain to them, because God has made it plain to them. For since the creation of the world, God's invisible qualities—his eternal power and divine nature—have been clearly seen, being understood from what has been made, so that men are without excuse.

Colossians 1:15-17 He is the image of the invisible God, the firstborn over all creation. For by him all things were created: things in heaven and on earth, visible and invisible, whether thrones or powers or rulers or authorities; all things were created by him and for him.

God's answer for all of the controversy about design vs. evolution is found in Isaiah 40:28 "Do you not know? Have you not heard? The LORD is the everlasting God, The Creator of the ends of the earth. He will not grow tired or weary, and his understanding no one can fathom."

No man can fathom how great God is, and therefore, sadly, man chooses to stay within himself and reject the magnificence of the God of the universe. Talk about the pride and arrogance of an evolutionist. I should know; I was one of them. It wasn't until I was willing to start afresh and research this whole issue myself, that my eyes were opened to the truth.

I soon found, in my own journey, that everyone has biases or presuppositions that affect how they look at the world, as well as what they see under a microscope. A creationist researcher would look at the complexity and the beauty of a single cell and marvel not only at the order, detail and the function of that cell, but at its Creator, as well. An evolutionist can look under the same microscope, and be amazed at the detail and how many millions of years it must have taken for this cell to randomly form itself. Why the different responses? Both cannot be correct. Both are swayed by a bias. The question is: Which one is reflecting truth? Where are they getting their information?

As a professor at Indiana University Medical School, Dr. Jim Williams teaches anatomy and is also a scientific researcher. He is brilliant and was taught through the years, as are most biology students, that evolution was scientific. He believed it until he was challenged to rethink his position. The following story is how he found the Intelligent Designer to be the God of the Scriptures, and what some of today's issues are regarding the creation/evolution debate.

Jim's Story. Growing up, I always loved nature and wanted to be a scientist, so it was natural for me to major in biology in college, and to head off to graduate school after that. Whatever faith in God that I had as a youth evaporated over those years, so that during the time of my post-doctoral research training, I was functionally an atheist, even though I do not remember thinking through much philosophy or religion during that period.

It was shortly after that, in my first faculty position at a college in South Carolina, when my wife said that she wanted to start taking the kids to Sunday school. I remember thinking that it was all pretend, and it wouldn't hurt me to go along just to keep peace in the family. However, I do remember quite a few Sundays when I went to the office, but something happened to me during those times that I did go to church. I began to become intrigued with the Bible; I started reading it every night. I didn't have anyone to talk to about it, and the church that we were in was not very helpful for someone wanting to learn about the Bible. Nonetheless, as the months went by, I grew in hunger for that knowledge.

By the time we moved to Indianapolis, we were dedicated churchgoers, and began looking for a church. We ended up in a Sunday school class that had an excellent Bible teacher. I remember being irritated with him, because he seemed so confident about what he taught. I kept going because, for the first time in my quest for answers, I was in an environment that I felt comfortable in asking questions, as well as learning the material.

That first winter was a great time of change for me. In addition to learning a lot from the Sunday school class, I discovered Christian radio and read a wide variety of Christian books. As the months went by, I had come to see myself as a sinner worthy of hell, who nonetheless, was saved by the sacrifice of Jesus Christ on my behalf. I don't remember much about the process, but it included a lot of study of the Scriptures. I remember being impacted from the Sermon on the Mount and doing a lot of searching into what the Good News actually means. I soon became a believer in Jesus Christ, and that spring was my first real celebration of Easter, and it was wonderful.

I found myself in a most unusual predicament: I was a professional biologist, doing research in a medical school and also a follower of Jesus Christ, with a growing trust in the Scriptures. It wasn't long until I began to feel the tension between the two.

I started investigating the creation/evolution controversy, and discovered several things right away. First, much of what I had learned as a biology student was less well-supported than I had thought. In brief, the advent of molecular biology in the 1960s has made it harder to imagine how life could have originated from a "primordial soup," and it has also made Darwin's theory harder to accept. For example, Darwinian Theory relies on variation among living things. Darwin thought that variation was continuous, so that the steps in the evolution of something (like a wing, or an eye) could happen through a long series of very tiny changes. That is macro-evolution. It turns out, though, that living things do not vary in that way. Indeed, even changes in the function of proteins—the building blocks of our bodies—almost always require "jumps" in protein structure.

To give an example, some proteins are enzymes, like the ones that digest our food. For evolution to change an enzyme into a "better" enzyme, the process must involve more than just changing the existing enzyme bit by bit, with the change of each little bit making the enzyme slightly better than it was before. You can't improve an enzyme very much by that process. Rather, you need to change the enzyme more dramatically, taking away big chunks of the protein, or adding more big chunks. This is not "smooth variation," but rather, "jumps" in structure. Such jumps in protein structure do not happen by simple variation as Darwin imagined it, and modern evolutionists have not been able to propose ways that this could have happened at the genesis (beginning) of life on our planet.

If you think about the odds of the molecules of life coming into being through a large number of such random events, it would take an irrational leap of faith to believe that life could begin on any planet through random arrangements of molecules. Yet many intelligent people believe exactly that. They trust that the universe is composed only of matter and energy, and put their faith in that, presuming that they must have come into being by some series of chance events.

Of course, it is not just molecules that are unlikely to appear by chance. Molecular biology continues to discover more multi-protein structures and processes that are obvious examples of "irreducible complexity" (as in Behe's book "Darwin's Black Box"). The processes inside of our cells are amazingly complex, with each process requiring multiple steps and multiple proteins, such that it is very hard to imagine how they could have come into being by any sort of unguided genesis. The more science learns about our bodies, the more complex the story gets. Darwin had no idea of how complicated living things are, and I suspect that his conclusions would have been very different if he had known the simplest molecular biology!

Despite this, I have seen that my colleagues are largely unable to see these problems as significant. It is as if they are thinking, "Matter and energy are all there is, so evolution must have happened, even if we don't have a clear idea of how it could have happened." Frankly, we biologists do not learn enough philosophy in school to see how to think about things like this.

Another problem my colleagues have (and I had) is confusing what is called micro-evolution with macro-evolution. Micro-evolution does, indeed, occur. We can see changes in animals and plants over time, and the scientists who study these things are discovering that some species even set themselves up for change, by carrying out sophisticated swapping of their own DNA, apparently to maximize change over a few generations, to enhance the survival of offspring. Changes that have been observed include the alteration of color in moth populations, recovery of lost enzyme functions in bacteria to enable them to resist antibiotics, and changes in beak dimensions in bird populations.

You will see these examples of micro-evolution used in the newspaper and television to "prove" that evolution happens. But micro-evolution does not bring into existence anything new. With micro-evolution the moths are still moths, and the bacteria still bacteria.

Macro-evolution is the process of new things (wings, eyes) and new creatures coming into being. Such a process has never been seen to occur. Its existence is inferred by evolutionists from fossils and from the similarity in DNA among living things. But fossils could have come from creatures buried in the past (such as in a flood) and DNA similarities among living things can simply indicate that they were created out of the same "workshop!" As we saw above, life could not have come into being without some outside influence, so there is no need to invoke macro-evolution for anything.

Some Christians want to believe in God and evolution, too. We can understand the reasons for this: No one wants to look uneducated in our society, and if you don't believe in macro-evolution, you are quickly labeled as foolish and backward in our culture. So, Christians try to put evolution and God together, saying that God created through evolution. The idea of God creating through evolution creates more problems than it solves. If God created through evolution, then death and suffering existed from the beginning of creation, because evolution (both micro and macro-evolution) occurs through the death of some, and the survival of others. If death and suffering were part of the creation of life, then most of the Bible has to be thrown out as badly wrong. Indeed, the very idea of Jesus coming to give us "life" becomes absurd, as the very definition of life is changed.

Christians who embrace evolution end up inventing a God-guided evolution that is very different from what evolutionists believe. And the price of this is a loss of most (if not all) of biblical theology. The stakes of this are high. If you accept evolution, you lose the God of Jesus Christ. I am not stating this too dramatically. For those Christians who struggle with these issues intellectually, I recommend a book by D. Russell Humphreys, "Starlight and Time."

From the history of science, one can see that, over and over again, scientists were set on a certain way of looking at the universe, only to have that overturned by new theories. We, as Christians, need not fear the discoveries of science. Rather, we must simply wait, and eventually the truth will be known: God created, just as He said.

How do we then respond to those who make us feel inadequate for believing in the biblical account of creation? As Dr. Williams alluded, this shaming not only comes from those in universities, but often from those in the church, as well. As long as churches think that they must mimic the world's philosophy, afraid to teach moral absolutes and the reliability of the Scriptures, they will continue to be in trouble.

Acts 17:11 Now the Bereans were of more noble character than the Thessalonians, for they received the message with great eagerness and examined the Scriptures every day to see if what Paul said was true.

Those of us in the church must be more like the Bereans in searching the Scriptures for the truth. If you, as a believer in Christ, have taken someone else's word for framing your belief in evolution instead of studying for yourself, then you are doing yourself and your church a huge disservice. The Church has become soft, as few as 2 percent, according to Josh McDowell, can give the reason for why they believe. As a result, many Christian leaders, teachers and students are intimidated by unbelieving professionals who do not believe because no one has given them a reason to believe. If these people would get serious about studying they would find that the Bible is true, and in this case that, yes, God did create the world Himself, with no help from evolution!

I would encourage those who profess to be believers, to study this subject before engaging in any debate. When you have studied up and understand the issues, you may be interested in using the following questions in your conversations with evolutionists. The following are proposed by Tom Foltz, a researcher and author who worked at NASA. He suggests several questions for you to ask those who are adamant in their stance of macro-evolution.

A brief summary of three of them follows:

1. Was there oxygen or no oxygen at the time the first cell evolved? If "yes," then free-oxygen would reduce or tear down an organism, not allowing that first weak cell to survive. If "no," then, life is without oxygen. How did it evolve? If we have oxygen we have no organic compounds, but if we don't have oxygen we have none either.[2] If either answer (a "yes" or a "no") leads to macro-evolution not being possible, then what else could it be but creation?

2. Does life come from non-life? The idea of spontaneous generation is the belief that life comes from non-life. This was disproved in the 1800s by Louis

Pasteur. The present law of biogenesis states that life only comes from pre-existing life.

If thousands of scientists have designed carefully planned experiments to create life from something nonliving, and yet have failed miserably every time, how in the world can we be expected to believe that nature did it by using accidents, chance and blind forces?[3]

In a summary of 1967 Nobel Prize winner Dr. George Wald's article entitled "The Origin of Life," there are only two possibilities as to how life arose. One is spontaneous generation arising to evolution; the other is a supernatural, creative act of God. There is no third possibility. Spontaneous generation (life from non-life) was scientifically disproved years ago by Louis Pasteur, Lazzaro Spallanzani, Francesco Redi and others, but that leaves us to only one conclusion: that life arose as a supernatural creative act of God. I will not accept that philosophically because I do not want to believe in God. Therefore, I choose to believe in that which I know is scientifically impossible: spontaneous generation arising to evolution.[4]

3. How did sex evolve? Which came first—asexual reproduction or sexual reproduction? Asexual reproduction is when an organism produces one or more clones of itself, such as by fission or budding. Sexual reproduction needs both a qualified male and female for reproduction. A mate MUST exist at the same time and place! Why would there be a need for sexual reproduction when one is already reproducing by itself?

"The evolution of sex is one of the major unsolved problems of biology. Even those with enough hubris to publish on the topic often freely admit that they have little idea of how sex originated or is maintained. It is enough to give heart to creationists," according to Michael Rose (Rose believes in macro-evolutionism).[5]

"Sex is something of an embarrassment to evolutionary biologists. Textbooks understandably skirt the issue, keeping it a closely guarded secret," says Kathleen McAuliffe (McAuliffe believes in macro-evolutionism).[6]

"It turns out that sex is a big puzzle for Darwinian theory. In fact, a literal interpretation of the theory predicts that sexual reproduction should not exist. Here's the problem. Given two organisms, if both are asexual, both can reproduce. If both are sexual, only one (the female) can bear young. A little math shows that asexual organisms should rapidly outbreed sexual ones and dominate the world. But since sexual species actually dominate, Darwinism has some explaining to do. In the past century, dozens of guesses have been made as to why, against straightforward expectations, sex predominates," states Dr. Michael Behe.[7] [*Note: Macro-evolutionists typically indicate mutations and sexual recombinations to explain this, but without any operational science validation.*]

These questions reflect the issue of this ongoing evolution/creation or intelligent design debate. It simply makes no sense from a science perspective to believe in evolution. You can see from the above quotes that scientists are admitting that evolution does not fit with even operational science, but yet they choose to believe it because they refuse to believe in a God who created. Research into macro-evolution says that it never existed in the past, nor the present or the future. It has been proven to be scientifically and mathematically impossible.

To those who say otherwise, I challenge you to present the evidence to prove what is written in this chapter to be wrong. I would encourage you to read such books as Michael Behe's book "Darwin's Black Box," James Perloff's "The Case Against Darwin," or maybe Michael Denton's book "Evolution: A Theory in Crisis." These books will give you greater insight of the real issues surrounding this debate.

"In the beginning, God created the heavens and the earth." God wasted no time in setting the record straight and He continues each and every day, through the beauty of a sunset and the laughter of a child. He is the Lord God of the universe—Creator of time and space and all that is, was and will be. He is the Intelligent Designer who created you. You are not an accident, but rather, a work of God's art. We are designed in the image of God, so that we can have a personal relationship with God through Jesus. He has designed us to be men and women of purpose who will not shy away from speaking truth to a deaf world. :: :: ::

:: **What God?**

CLASSROOM COMBAT ::

chapter 9

:: What God?

in the spring of every high school senior's life, something

tremendous happens. When that final diploma is given out and the graduation caps are flung into the air, a new life begins. For some, it means getting a job. For others, plans of further education start to become reality. These graduates will be living away from home, rooming with a new roommate, meeting friends and taking classes that will build a foundation for whatever line of work lies in the future. If you are one of those individuals venturing into new academic horizons, these words will be especially helpful to you as you encounter a barrage of worldly thinking. I encourage you to read this chapter to help prepare and educate yourself for what lies ahead. Keep in mind that all institutions vary in a multitude of ways. Beyond the obvious differences in size, shape, climate and course offerings, there is, however, much that they have in common.

I had a conversation with Abby Nye, who wrote "Fish Out of Water," during an Anchorsaway class. She spoke to the students to prepare them for what might happen once they left home. Parts of my conversation with her, as well as other former students' experiences, will follow.

> **Abby's Story.** Freshman orientation was not what I expected it to be. I expected it to be a time when I would go and find my classes, buy my books and they'd tell us about the cool places to study, where to eat and not eat, all that stuff. And I quickly found out that it was a fast-paced, indoctrination scheme. They had activities that were mandatory. Although I learned after the fact, that if it's not for a grade, it can't really be mandatory. So, you don't have to go to every activity that's on the schedule, so feel free to skip those you don't want to attend. Some of the activities had a slant. I thought, "Is this just a coincidence?" No, they are trying to brainwash you, in a sense. And they do it so quickly that you don't have time to think about it and process it all. For me, it felt like I was basically being held hostage for three or four days, while those leading the program were attempting to reprogram our brains on matters of moral relativism, tolerance, gay/lesbian/transgender rights, Postmodernism and New Age spirituality.

They like to do it in a fun way, too. We would go to skits about homosexuality. The message would be that homosexuality is normal. If you don't think it's normal, something is wrong with you; you're weird. Other skits would be about drugs: it's okay to do drugs. It's not okay to snoop around and ask if your roommate's doing them, because they live their own life. Also, they talk about drinking and sex. It was just a given that that goes on at college and that's okay. And the message would be that everyone has premarital sex, so when you do, please use a condom. I quickly grew very tired of this Welcome Week and I thought, "Okay, it's already the first week and classes haven't started yet, and I do not like this place too much!" I decided to skip the last activity called "Interactive Rape Seminar," just because.

The shock waves from freshman orientation had barely subsided when I received a second jolt. Required reading in my English class included not Shakespeare or Milton, but essays on why America deserved the terrorist attacks of 9/11, why we should listen to the Columbine killers, and why "under God" should be removed from the Pledge of Allegiance.

In another class, the professor had given us an article called "Cutting God in Half." It said that if God exists, He cannot be all loving, all knowing and all powerful. Our assignment was to analyze the article. I was like, "Okay, great, this is about religion. I'm okay with this. I have a strong worldview." The instructions to the assignment said we could use our personal beliefs and our own convictions to write this paper. "Okay, great! I can write it from the Christian worldview." Now, knowing that I was at a secular college and that the professor was not a Christian, I wasn't going to use Bible verses, but I did write it from the Christian worldview perspective. I got the paper back and there were 33 comments on it, none of which were pertaining to grammar, style or how I wrote the paper poorly. I got a B- on the paper, and I knew that it wasn't a B- paper. The professor wrote comments that were all directed toward Christianity.

I knew that something wasn't right and that it wasn't a fair grade. I felt that he was baiting us. This was the assignment that he chose; he picked this article and specifically told us that we could use our beliefs to write a response to it. I knew he was looking for something to kind of start a fight. So I arranged a meeting with the head of the English department and my professor to talk about this paper. We had a 45-minute meeting, and what it came down to is that the head of the department told me that "you cannot use the Bible in academic circles, because it's regarded as a book of myth." That's what they told me—straight up.

I pointed out to them that if I were an Islamic student and I was using the Koran, I didn't think we would be here having this meeting; that I thought perhaps the only thing that's not being tolerated here is Christianity.

Abby is not the only student who experienced a bias against Christianity. Joshua Birk wrote an article for BreakPoint Worldview[1] entitled Finding God at Michigan. In it he said: "I don't completely remember the first day of the philosophy class. Nor do I clearly recall the second. It was a 9:00 a.m. class. But I clearly remember when, a couple of weeks into the course, my professor announced that we would be discussing Thomas Aquinas' First Cause argument, a famous argument for the existence of God. I was excited. This is why I had chosen philosophy. I wanted to probe the deep thoughts of wizened, graying professors and hash out life's big questions with other students who had a "love of wisdom." My lofty visions of philosophical studies were quickly deflated as the professor took the first five minutes to outline the argument, and the next 45 to rip it to shreds.

"There I was, foolishly thinking my professor was going to prove the logic of Christianity and put the rest of my unenlightened class in their place. As the weeks progressed, I began to feel more on my own. I had Christian support outside the classroom, but in the classroom, Christians were an endangered species."

The first thing to know about universities and colleges, both secular and Christian, is that there is generally an overwhelming liberal bias afloat in academia. Our goal is not to fight each professor that we sit under, but rather be someone who knows what we believe and who can respond with gentleness and respect when we speak. Most of our experiences will be "seed planting" experiences: it is our goal to speak truth that causes others to think. It is also important to listen and learn from those with whom we differ.

Alexandria's Story. As a freshman at a small, Midwestern private university, I was faced with a number of challenges that had escaped me at an equally small, Midwestern Christian high school. One of the biggest challenges, and ultimately the greatest refresher, was the wide range of beliefs and backgrounds represented. My first eye-opening experience occurred in a biology class where the professor openly expressed his staunch views of evolution. I was deeply troubled by the class and sought advice from fellow Christian students, roommates and family. I was given all the advice that would be expected: to remain friendly but firm, to use the opportunity to be a light in a dark place, and most importantly, to share my own beliefs with my professor.

The story, in itself, is not a marked success. The biology professor made no apparent change, but I did grow to respect him as a person and as a professor. However, the story is God's success. As Christians in a secular world we are commanded to be trusting witnesses, those who share our faith boldly and then believe in God's power to change hearts.

Please don't be surprised to know that a vast majority of professors are atheists who do not like Christians. Notice that I did not say Christianity. Why? I believe it is because much of their bias against Christianity is defined by the Christians that are in their classrooms. From talking with many of these professors, I have learned most are quick to point out that those who do dare say something about their faith and Jesus can rarely, if ever, give reasons as to why those things they believe are true and reasonable. Most professors are annoyed with the shallowness of their thinking. Sadly, I believe that their opinions of the Christian responses are not far off. Professors get away with much, because they know that most who initially take a stand for their faith in the classroom, cower when challenged. This lack of readiness by Christians gives skeptical professors license to provoke believers, often times to the point of believers walking away from their faith. One professor admitted his joy in breaking a student out of the "cuffs of their controlling, traditional and simplistic faith."

More of Abby's Story. Oftentimes, I was the only one speaking up in defense of Christianity. And I would look around and see faces of students that I also saw in Campus Crusade, that I knew were Christians. Yet, I was the only one speaking up. So, my challenge to Christian students at secular schools is to speak up.

Someone told me that courage is not the absence of fear, but it's speaking up in spite of fear. And that's so true, because it's scary. Sometimes I was like "I can't believe I'm doing this; I'm speaking up. I mean, I'm not that gutsy." With God enabling you, you can, you should speak up. Even if you can't speak up, you can stand up next to somebody. It's nice to have somebody saying, "I'm behind you." But, "way behind you" doesn't help. You know, they kind of need to be there with you, encouraging you. It is encouraging to hear from a student, even if it is after class, just that they did agree with you or they support you, because that keeps you going and gives you the confidence to do it again.

In the classroom or out, the Christian who stands up for biblical moral truths will, no doubt, be called "intolerant" or "judgmental."

Tolerance in our culture has come to mean that we all have different beliefs and different value systems. Therefore, all ideas are equal. Such belief statements are straight out of a Postmodern primer. There are no absolute truths, nor moral absolutes. Anything goes. Beware to the one who stands up and says that there are moral absolutes, because they will be called intolerant.

It is easy to talk Postmodern, but to live it is another story. Suppose you found your roommate's keys and took his car out for a drive. You brought it back when the gas tank was on empty. You had left food and spilled drinks in it. Your roommate had to cancel a date, because you had taken his car. If you both were true Postmodernists, the owner would say that it was fine that you did what you did, because that was what you wanted to do. He did not want to be intolerant of your value system. The driver would have offered no apology, because he didn't have to give a reason for anything! You can only imagine what life would be like if our culture really did live out its complete tolerance. Mass chaos would break out, jails would be empty and, no doubt, so would your bank account, home and garage. No culture could survive if people lived in such a way. But yet, the Christian will be tagged as intolerant for making a truth claim.

No doubt, if the Christian is a truth teller, he or she will also be labeled judgmental. It is true that we are never to judge where someone is going to spend eternity. That can change in the last second of life, making it the Lord's job. However, Ephesians 5:11 says, "Have nothing to do with the fruitless deeds of darkness, but rather expose them." We are called to speak out and be light to darkness.

Another issue that Christians should learn to respond to is the false idea that Christianity is intolerant and judgmental. The truth is that Christianity is the most tolerant and nonjudgmental religion that there is in the world. We are called to love all people, because God loves all people and calls them all to Him. Be it a Jew, Muslim, Buddhist, Hindu, male, female, gay or straight, anyone from any other religion can come to Jesus of the Scriptures, and confess that Jesus Christ is God and that He died for their sins. They will become God's child at that very point in time. Jesus Christ died for all who sinned. All are loved, but not all people are His children.

Be encouraged by the following Scriptures:

Acts 2:21 And everyone who calls on the name of the Lord will be saved.

Acts 4:10-12 It is by the name of Jesus Christ of Nazareth, whom you crucified but whom God raised from the dead, that this man stands before you healed. He is 'the stone you builders rejected, which has become the capstone.' Salvation is found in no one else, for there is no other name under heaven given to men by which we must be saved.

2 Peter 3:9 The Lord is not slow in keeping his promise, as some understand slowness. He is patient with you, not wanting anyone to perish, but everyone to come to repentance.

Be confident, but don't be surprised when the world turns on you (1 John 3:13). God calls us to love our enemies. We are also called to love all people different from ourselves—even if they don't love us. It's easy to love people that love you, but it's quite another thing to love someone who really can't stand you. By love, I mean to show kindness and respect. Pointing your finger at someone and telling them that they are going straight to hell is wrong, and is not in any way supported by God. That kind of behavior fuels the fire of contempt toward Christians, and pushes people farther away from Christ, the Redeemer.

We, as believers, were not born believers. We are the recipients of God's grace, because somebody cared and loved us into a relationship with Christ. We are saved by grace, and it is by God's grace that we can live in a world that has gone completely mad! Should we not extend a hand of grace to others, who are lost? :: :: ::

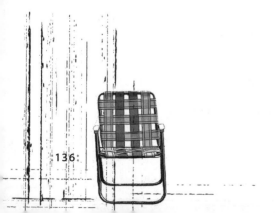

DEADLY QUESTIONS ::

chapter 10

when I first became a believer and was trying to make

sense of my new-found life, I bumped into a friend who had heard that I had become one of those "born-again freaks." He couldn't believe that I would give in to such nonsense and said, "I always thought that you were a lot smarter than that!"

"Christianity is not garbage, nor is it a covey of freaks; it is the truth, pure and simple!" I said, thinking that my response would put an end to this conversation that was going nowhere.

"Anybody from any religion could make that claim," he responded. I was dumbfounded. He was right and I did not have a response for his comment. I was so upset that I had let the Lord down by not being better prepared.

1 Peter 3:15-17 But in your hearts set apart Christ as Lord. Always be prepared to give an answer to everyone who asks you to give the reason for the hope that you have. But do this with gentleness and respect, keeping a clear conscience, so that those who speak maliciously against your good behavior in Christ may be ashamed of their slander.

I am sure that I am not the only one who has been caught unprepared when confronted with questions regarding the truth of Christianity. I thank God for that conversation, because it made me think through and prepare a response that would cause the questioner to think about their own belief system. I was determined that the next time it happened (and it did), that I would be ready to give an answer with gentleness and respect.

The very best defense of the Christian faith is to know the truth, really know it, not just being familiar with it, but know it. Then we can engage in a conversation that not only will answer someone's questions, but will also afford us the opportunity of gracefully challenging their own belief system.

The following four questions are extremely effective questions to ask those who are attacking or challenging your faith. They are also useful when you want to point out the error of thinking in someone else's point of view.[1] I strongly encourage you to memorize these and prepare to use them whenever you encounter adversity, be it in a classroom, during lunch, at a meeting or just hanging out with friends. You will find that, as you familiarize yourself with these questions, they will become a natural part of your conversations without having to work at it.

1. What do you mean by that? Any time that you wish to get into a discussion with someone, make sure that the terms are defined. Oftentimes the discussion will end here if there is a misunderstanding in terms. You will fast weed out those who just want to argue and have no clue about the issue.

If someone says, "Only idiots would believe that God inspired the writing of the Bible," your response might be, "What do you mean by 'idiots' and what do you mean by 'inspired'?"

2. How do you know that is true? Surprisingly, most people believe things for which they have absolutely no evidence. Try this question out on someone with strong opinions and be ready for a fascinating discussion.

In this particular case the question would be, "Do you know all the 'idiots' in the world? If not, then how can you make such a statement?" Then ask, "How do you know that the Bible is not inspired by God? What is your evidence?"

3. Where do you get your information? When someone makes a radical claim, you should always ask detailed questions about how they know what they know. Before long, you will get to the end of their knowledge and will be on even terms in the discussion.

"Have you read the Bible? What exactly are the verses that you are holding in question? Have you considered the prophecies in the Bible, all 2,000 of them? How many of those have come true? Is that mathematically possible or probable?" Chances are that you will not get beyond the first question. I would encourage them to do their homework and you might offer them some good sources for truth, like those in Chapter 3 of this book!

4. What happens if you are wrong? It is one thing to claim a belief, and yet another to stake your life on it. The most important question that can be asked in life is, "Where do you go when you die, and what happens if you are wrong?"

When dealing with the argument that God did not inspire the Bible to be written, a good rebuttal to this might be, "If by chance you are wrong about

Christians and about the Bible, then consider that the Bible tells the story of God's love for all people and offers, to all who choose to believe in Him, eternal life in heaven with Him. For those of you who do not believe in Jesus and His sacrificial death on the cross that paid the price for your sins, then God will give you the desire of your heart, and you will live forever without Him. In spite of your unbelief, God loves you and wants you, too, to believe in Him. Are you content in being where you are or are you interested in at least entertaining the idea that there is a God who loves you?"

Last week I was talking with a youth pastor, and he mentioned that he disagreed with the idea of biblical creationism that I teach in the Anchorsaway curriculum. I asked him with what it was that he disagreed. He said that he believed that God started creation, but then evolution kicked in. If you recall from my earlier chapter that discusses creation, this is what is known as theistic evolution.

Knowing that the biblical account of creation is true in its entirety, I wanted to argue with him, but instead asked him what he meant by evolution. He said that he believed that it was a combination of random chance and God. I then asked him how he knew it was true. He said he had received this information from one of his college professors at a well-known Christian college in Chicago. "I know what your professor believes, but what you are telling me is that your source for rejecting God's Word is one teacher's opinion. Don't you think you owe it to yourself, the Lord and your students to look into this issue for yourself? I will give you some books to study if you would like, but please, would you study it for yourself?"

Sadly, that was the end of the conversation. To this day, he continues to pass on what was passed on to him; that God was only a part of the creation story, thus undermining the veracity of the Scriptures and all that is found within. James 3:1-2 "Not many of you should presume to be teachers, my brothers, because you know that we who teach will be judged more strictly."

Practice these questions on your friends, and then on those who are attacking your ideas. Then, have your friends turn the tables on you, and ask you the deadly questions to some of your truth claims. This is a great exercise to build up your confidence, not only in confronting others, but in your own faith, as well! :: :: ::

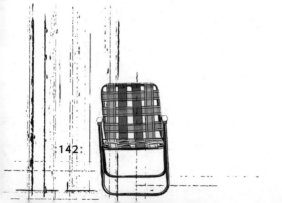

SATAN'S GAMES ::

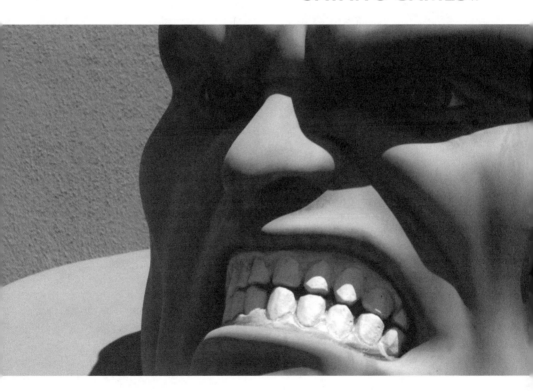

chapter 11

:: **What God?**

with all of the evil in the world, with all the Satanic movies and with the rising of occultic groups like Wicca, one would think that most people would believe that Satan is real. The majority of people, however, do not believe that Satan is a living being, but think that he is just a symbol or an evil force.

If Scripture is true, and we know that it is, then Satan is not only real, but active in the world today. Writings of Ezekiel 28:11-19, Isaiah 14:12-20 and Luke 10:18 tell us of Satan's fall from heaven. Like so many of us, Satan's pride got the best of him and he wanted to be worshiped, rather than to worship the One True God. Like most deceivers, not only does the leader convince himself or herself to believe something that is not true, but he or she takes many others down the path of deception. Satan wanted to be worshiped just like God, and because of his lack of belief and his deceiving nature, God kicked Satan, along with a third of the angels, out of heaven and to earth.

The New Testament is full of references to the names of Satan including: Tempter, Counterfeiter, Destroyer, Liar, Murderer, Prince of Demons, Lawless One, Devil, Serpent and the Evil One. The names Satan, Devil, demons and evil spirits are mentioned 165 times in the New Testament. Jesus referred to Satan by name several times. There is no doubt that Satan was real in Jesus' day and there is no reason to think that he is not real today.

How does he work? A direct line to Satan is through the occult. The occultists believe that an infinite "force" pervades the universe, and those initiated into its secrets can use the force to their own ends.[1] It is blatantly the work of Satan and his demons. Tools used in the occult are tarot cards, crystals, Ouija boards, charms, secret oaths, spirit guides, astrology, transcendental meditation, yoga and labyrinths. Occultic groups include Wicca/Witchcraft, Vampirism, Shamanism and the New Age.

A more secretive way that Satan works is through cults. The definition of a "cult," from a Christian perspective, is a group of people centered on the false teachings of a leader who claims that he/she is uniquely called by God. A cult requires at least two people: a leader and a follower. There are, in the United States, about 5,000 different types of cults. Some cults include only a few members, and you likely have never heard of them. Others, like the Mormons (called The Church of Jesus Christ of Latter Day Saints), are so large that they have become a household name.

Scripture tells us that Satan is constantly at work "looking for someone to devour" (1 Peter 5:8). Ultimately, he is the originator of any philosophy, religion or belief system that runs counter to God's truth, often twisting reality so that it has a certain attraction to those who are unaware of his schemes. He will always mix his lies with some truth, even quoting Scripture, if necessary. Thousands of churched individuals are unknowingly drawn into cults. Satan is not a respecter of age, race, religion, social status or wealth. He will go after anyone and everyone. The most vulnerable are those who do not have their minds set on Christ, the Son of God, or who are ignorant of the writings of the Bible. That is why this subject is so critical.

It is important to know some of the common characteristics of a cult. The following is a brief list of things you might want to consider before you join a group that professes to be Christian. Not all groups possess all of these characteristics, but any one of them should be a warning to you to stay away from them.

:: They will often reveal new truths that supersede or contradict the Bible.

:: They have new interpretations of Scripture that are used to justify certain cultic beliefs.

:: They use a non-biblical source of authority, whose sacred writings or authority often supersede the Bible, and worship another "Jesus," whom they see as a prophet, but not as God.

:: They will present a new definition, or complete denial, of the Trinity.

:: They believe that salvation is not by grace, but by works.

:: The cult will revolve around a central leader who often will claim to have new revelations from God.

Our Postmodern culture is built on different versions of truth, making us vulnerable to the infiltration of various cults and false religions. Sadly, these numerous cults, including Mormonism, have seduced millions of people into embracing their brand of truth. As we become aware of the different cults that exist, our vigilance will keep us from being persuaded to believe a lie, even within our own churches (See 2 Timothy 4:1-5). Furthermore, we will then be able to bring others into the light of God's truth.

Let's take a look at Mormonism. Why? It is one of the fastest growing counterfeit Christian religions in America today. More than 11 million people are members and more than 63,000 are full-time missionaries. They are out knocking on doors and are extremely active on college campuses, which they see as breeding grounds for future Mormon members.

Agusta and Dan Harting were Mormons for 15 years. Agusta speaks to several different groups, including Anchorsaway. The following is her testimony of how she became a Mormon, what it entailed, and how she escaped from it. Today, she and her husband have a ministry to Mormons and to those in other cults, as well.

Agusta Harting's Story. I was born and raised in Reykjavik, Iceland. Although my parents were not active in our Lutheran church, they still made me go to catechism (religious instructions) to be confirmed into the church at age 14. I came away from confirmation nearly as ignorant of the Christian faith as I had been before, only now I considered myself to be a "Christian!"

The years passed, and when I turned 19, I met my husband, Dan, an American Navy officer who was stationed in Iceland for a few years. We moved to the U.S. and began raising our family of five children. Dan, who was raised a nominal Presbyterian, did not know much more about the Bible than I did. We carefully avoided going to church, politely declining if anybody we knew invited us to come along with them.

After 10 years of marriage we were not happy, to say the least. I was beginning to feel empty and unfulfilled, no matter what worldly success we were enjoying. I had a very glamorous TV and modeling career, and Dan was fast climbing up the corporate ladder in a prestigious firm, making fistfuls of money as we went along. We had everything the world has to offer, but still I felt something was horribly missing in our lives.

:: Missionaries

One day, two Mormon missionaries showed up at our door. I eagerly invited them in, and they proceeded to teach me all about their church. I agreed to have them give me "The Six Discussions," as they call them; I was genuinely interested. Little did I know that I would not really be learning much about the bizarre teachings of this cult, but that I would be systematically led down the proverbial "primrose path" to deception, thinking this was all "Christianity," in its purest form. The slick program I was being presented was carefully designed to make me agree quickly to be baptized into the "only true church," as Mormons call their Church of Jesus Christ of Latter Day Saints, or "The Mormon Church," as it is nicknamed by them and others.

At this point you might be wondering, "Why is Mormonism so bad? Don't they call themselves Christians?" Please remember that I bear no grudge against any particular member of the Mormon Church. Like most other cultists, Satan has blinded them to the truth of the real Gospel of Jesus Christ, and he holds them bound in this deception, which is both tricky and subtle. It is because I care about Mormons that I would have you be better equipped in witnessing to them about the real Jesus Christ of the Bible, whom they think they already represent.

:: The beginnings
The Mormons taught me that their movement, to which they refer as "The Restoration," began in 1820, when a young man who was 14 years old allegedly went into the woods to pray about which of all the churches in his vicinity he should join. His name was Joseph Smith, Jr.

I was told that no sooner had young Smith begun to pray, than a power so evil that he thought it would destroy him, seized upon him and bound his tongue. And just when he thought he would surely die, a pillar of light, brighter than the noonday sun, appeared above him. In the light stood two white-haired men, whom we are to assume to be God, the Father and his Son, Jesus Christ. Mormons call this event "The First Vision," and hang all the existence for their church and its "restored gospel" upon it! (Naturally, I had no idea that there are nine versions to this story, each differing greatly from the others.)

The "official" version of this story records that the father and the son told Joseph Smith to join NONE of the churches found on the Earth, for they were ALL false! He was told that all statements of faith (creeds) in all of Christianity were a lie, false and abominable in God's sight. Also, that all those who professed faith in them were "liars."

After the Mormons told me this awesome story, they quietly and deliberately said, "Sister Harting, we bear you our testimony that these things we have told you are true. And, by the power of the Holy Ghost you can come to know that they are true, also." This "testimony" was borne to me more than 80 times in the following five discussions.

Later, they told me that Joseph Smith claimed that an angel had appeared in his bedroom, and told him that he (Joseph) would be the instrument that God would use in restoring the Gospel to the Earth. It had supposedly been lost when the original 12 apostles of Jesus Christ died. Because I was ignorant about the Bible, I did not know that the Gospel of Jesus Christ was never lost, but is clearly laid out in 1 Corinthians 15:1-5.

The "angel" told Joseph Smith that his name was Moroni, and that he and his people before him had lived on the American continent from 600 BC to 431 AD. Moroni, the son of Mormon, was supposedly a great warrior in his Earth life, but he had now become an angel. The story goes that this angel of light led Joseph Smith to a place on the hill above the Smith's farm, and told him to dig there for some gold plates with curious engravings upon them, which Mormons claim was "Reformed Egyptian" (a language which has never been known or heard of in all of history!).

Now the young elders gave me a copy of their famous book, "The Book of Mormon," and told me that it was the final fruit of Joseph's digging. By miraculous means, and with special "stones set in bows" found with the plates, he was allegedly able to translate the golden plates into English, and published in 1830 what is now known as "The Book of Mormon." He also established the Mormon Church that same year.

I asked if I could see the golden plates, but the elders answered that the angel had taken them to heaven, and that more plates would come forth some day. This sounded even fishier to me! But Satan is clever and cultic powers are very seductive. Those sweet elders implored me to pray about the truthfulness of the Book of Mormon. They simultaneously told me that the Bible had been translated so many times that it could have lost most of its meaning; it was definitely not a reliable book, according to them. On the contrary, Joseph Smith said in 1830 that The Book of Mormon was "the most correct book on Earth and a man can get closer to God by living by its precepts than by any other book." (I was not told that the B.O.M. had been changed in more than 3,900 places without footnotes!)[2]

"Sister Harting, all you have to do is pray about it, and then listen to your heart! If you feel a burning in your bosom, you will have prayed honestly and can know the book is true!" Foolishly, and contrary to biblical warnings, I put this deceptive formula to the test and thought perhaps that I had "felt something" in my bosom! The Bible says in Proverbs 28:26 (NKJV),

> "He who trusts in his own heart is a fool,
> But whoever walks wisely will be delivered."

Once I had convinced myself that the Book of Mormon was true, everything else fell into place like dominos. I was baptized by immersion by Mormon priests. I was told that only they had the authority to baptize anyone on earth. Peter, James and John, the Apostles of old, also supposedly came in person and ordained them to the Melchizedek Priesthood (even though the Bible declares in Hebrews 7 that Jesus ALONE holds this priesthood). When I asked about the date of this great event, the missionaries hemmed and hawed and said that Joseph Smith had forgotten to write down the date!

I now thought that I had finally become a Christian. My husband soon followed suit, as did my son, who was 8 years old, the only one of our children at the time to qualify for Mormon baptism by being "at the age of accountability."

Time passed quickly, and eventually, we became isolated from all former friends and relatives by being kept so busy in the church; we had no time for anything else. Soon, we began to prepare to go to the Mormon Secret Temple to be "sealed for time and all eternity." Mormons consider this vital for gaining Eternal Life. Space prohibits me from describing the temple ritual in much detail, but nonetheless, it shocked me to no end.[3]

I will say that during this ungodly ceremony, we received "secret names" and had to don ghoulish, Druid-like clothing, all in white, except for a bright green fig leaf apron which we had to wear throughout the ritual. Worthy Mormons are even buried in this ghastly costume. We were shown a film depicting a typical Christian minister who was in the employ of Satan, and the main doctrines of the Christian faith were mocked. However, since 1990, Mormons have deleted some of the objectionable things from the ceremony, in order to make it more acceptable. Those "oaths, signs and penalties" that we were made to perform had this intent: to give all our time, talents and earthly goods over to the Mormon

Church, as well as "our lives, if necessary." We were made to swear an oath never to reveal this "sacred" ritual!

:: Finding freedom

My family and I remained in the darkness of Mormonism until 1981. Then, God, by His infinite grace, allowed me to hear the REAL Gospel of Jesus Christ on the radio in Indianapolis, and I knew it was true! NOT because of my "feelings," or a "burning in the bosom," but because I carefully compared it with the Bible, God's ONLY authority on Earth! A short time later my husband, and every one of our children, left Mormonism. Most of our children are born again Christians today.

In 1981, God called me and my husband to serve Him in the capacity of missionaries to Mormons and other cultists, as well as equipping His church in how to reach Mormons for Christ. Eventually, Families Against Cults was formed and we are currently working hard to bring other lost souls into the precious Kingdom of God, while we await the return of our precious Lord, Jesus Christ. He has graciously allowed us to see hundreds of cultists brought "out of darkness into his wonderful light!" (1 Peter 2:9).

I think that one of the most important things that a Christian needs to know is that when someone is in a counterfeit Christian religion, the meaning of their words and phrases and those of the Christian faith and the Holy Bible can seem very similar, but they do not mean the same thing! So, many people get swept into cults because they are tricked into thinking that it is just another very friendly Church that loves families. Check out the following:

1. "God is my Father in Heaven."

Mormon meaning: God is a 6-foot, physical "exalted man." His name is "Elohim." Once only a mere human, he had to learn to become god. He has a father, and there are many gods above him. He is only the "god of this universe."[4]

Christian meaning: Even though He is a personal Being, God, the Father has never been human. He is the Creator, and we are the created. God has created the entire universe. He is the head of the Trinity and all things are subject to Him; there is nothing, and no one, who is above Him (Genesis 1:1; 1 Corinthians 15:27-28).

2. "Jesus Christ is God's Son."

Mormon meaning: Jesus Christ was a spirit baby born to Heavenly Father and one of his goddess wives, "Heavenly Mother." They named him "Jehovah." God is married to many women, and he cannot create anything from nothing. He had to have sex with his wife in order to produce Jesus pre-mortally, as well as all of humanity by the same method. Lucifer, the Devil, is also one of Jesus' "Spiritual Brothers."[5]

Christian meaning: Jesus, as God's Son, shares all of the qualities of God, Himself. He lacks nothing. As such, He never came into being because He has always been. In addition, Jesus has power over the Devil. The Devil has never been a spiritual equal of Jesus, as he is a fallen angel, and all angels are subject to Christ (Matthew 28:18; Luke 10:18-19; John 8:58; Colossians 1:15-18; Revelation 12:7-9).

3. "The Holy Ghost is the third member of the Godhead."

Mormon meaning: The Holy Ghost is a different god than Heavenly Father (Elohim). He has no physical body, and we do not know his name. He must not be confused with "The Holy Spirit," which is only like an impersonal electrical current.[6]

Christian meaning: In the history of Christianity, the title, "Holy Ghost," has frequently been interchangeable with the more common title, "Holy Spirit," when referring to the third member of the Trinity. They are not two separate entities, but instead, references to the same Being. The doctrine of the Trinity tells us that "God eternally exists as three persons, Father, Son and Holy Spirit, and each person is fully God, and there is one God."[7] Therefore, the Holy Spirit is not a different God; He is God. He is a personal Being who has been sent to give us regeneration and help us live in obedience to God (Matthew 28:19; John 3:5-8; Ephesians 4:30 – Note: Only a personal Being can be "grieved").

4. "Jesus Christ is my Savior and Lord."

Mormon meaning: Jesus (Jehovah) had to come to Earth to complete his test of godhood. While here, he was married (possibly a polygamist)[8] and sweat blood in Gethsemane in order to "atone" for mankind and assure that we would all "gain resurrection bodies" someday. He is our "Elder Brother,"[9] and we must imitate him in order to earn and merit Eternal Life.

Christian meaning: Jesus did not earn His deity; He has always been God (Genesis 1:1; John 1:1-3). Yes, 1 John 2:6 tells us we must imitate Jesus by walking as He did, but our obedience to Christ is not a means to salvation. Salvation is a gift of God, which comes through our faith in Jesus' atoning sacrifice of Himself on the cross for our sins (Ephesians 2:8-9; 1 John 2:2).

5. "Jesus was born of a virgin."

Mormon meaning: God (Elohim) came down to Earth and had literal sexual intercourse with his virgin daughter, Mary. She thus conceived the earthly body for Jesus (Jehovah).[10]

Christian meaning: The Bible tells us that the Holy Spirit, not God, the Father, was the One who impregnated the virgin, Mary (Matthew 1:18-21; Luke 1:30-35). This was not a physical act of intercourse, but rather, a miraculous act of conception through the Holy Spirit.

6. "Jesus Christ is God."

Mormon meaning: Jesus Christ is a god, one of possibly billions of gods. Mormons are forbidden to worship or pray to him. They are not to have a "personal relationship" with him.[11]

Christian meaning: The Trinity doctrine tells us that there is only one God, not multiple gods. As a part of the Trinity, Jesus possesses the same divine characteristics of God, the Father (John 8:58, 10:30). We are called to bow before Christ in worship and demonstrate our love for Him through our obedience to His commands (Philippians 2:9-11). Our personal relationship with Jesus is cultivated as we follow Him, in much the same way as He had a personal relationship with the 12 disciples during His three years of ministry on earth (John 10:27).

7. "Salvation is by God's grace through faith and works."

Mormon meaning: God only gives us the "grace" to be resurrected in a body of flesh and bone through Christ's sweating blood and death on the cross. Eternal Life, however, must be EARNED and merited through personal worthiness.[12] This is called Eternal Progression to godhood. This is every Mormon's goal. The slogan in Mormonism is: "As man is, God once was; as God is, man may become!"[13]

Christian meaning: Scripture tells us that we have been saved through faith in God's gift of grace (Ephesians 2:8-9). We are not saved through our own merits. God has called us to come under His authority. When we seek to elevate ourselves above God, we sin against Him. (See the stories of Eve in Genesis 3:1-6 and the Tower of Babel in Genesis 11:1-9.)

8. "I believe in heaven and hell."

Mormon meaning: Heaven: There are three heavens. They are called the Celestial, Terrestrial and Telestial Kingdoms.[14] Most Christians and unworthy Mormons only qualify for the second, or the Terrestrial.[15] Worthy Mormons, who have become gods and goddesses, inherit the Celestial Kingdom. They will beget spirit children and populate their own Earths and planets, just like Heavenly Parents did. The Telestial Kingdom is for the wicked, but still "glorious," according to Joseph Smith.

Hell: is only a temporary prison for all non-Mormons until the resurrection. Great missionary work is being performed there right now.[16]

Outer Darkness: is where the Devil and the demons go, as well as apostates who have left Mormonism and have become "Sons of Perdition." They remain there forever.

Christian meaning: The Bible speaks of only two eternal destinations for humanity—heaven or hell. They are both literal places, and Scripture does not suggest that there is more than one heaven. Hell is the place of eternal punishment for the wicked, while the righteous will enjoy eternal life in heaven (Matthew 25:46).

9. "I believe the Bible is true, as far as it is translated correctly."

Mormon meaning: The Bible was not translated correctly and there are many "plain and precious truths" missing in it, including whole books. According to Mormon Prophet Ezra T. Benson, it is not "big enough, nor good enough, to lead this [the Mormon] Church."

Christian meaning: The Bible is not only true, it is also without error. The three common tests for works of antiquity (Bibliographic, Internal and External) confirm the authenticity of the Bible. More importantly, Scripture itself proclaims that every word has come from God, Himself (2 Timothy 3:16-17; 2 Peter 1:20-21). Therefore, it is pure, perfect and true (Psalm 12:6, 119:96; Proverbs 30:5).[17] There is nothing that needs to be added or taken away from God's Word; it is all we need for salvation (Deuteronomy 4:2, 12:32; Proverbs 30:5-6; Revelation 22:18-19).

10. "I believe in all the gifts of the Holy Ghost."

> **Mormon meaning:** All spiritual gifts must be given from Joseph Smith, Jr., through the General Authorities of the Mormon Church, channeled down to the recipient by the laying on of hands by Mormon priests.[18]

> **Christian meaning:** Scripture tells us that all gifts come from God and are bestowed upon us by the Holy Spirit, Himself (James 1:17; 1 Corinthians 12:1-11).

I pray that all of you will clearly see the difference between Mormon teachings and the doctrine of the Christian faith!

Please remember, in spite of the same terminology, Mormons worship a false god; they proclaim another (false) Jesus, and they teach a false gospel! To see how seriously God considers this:

Galatians 1:6-9 (The Apostle Paul speaking) "I am astonished that you are so quickly deserting the one who called you by the grace of Christ and are turning to a different gospel—which is really no Gospel at all. Evidently some people are throwing you into confusion and are trying to pervert the Gospel of Christ. But even if we or an angel from heaven should preach a Gospel other than the one we preached to you, let him be eternally condemned! As we have already said, so now I say again: If anybody is preaching to you a Gospel other than what you accepted, let him be eternally condemned!"

Monica was a student of Anchorsaway and especially enjoyed hearing Agusta Harting speak. She had a Mormon friend who lived in another city. Monica decided to begin an email exchange with him. Her purpose was to challenge him to think again about what he had been taught about Mormonism and to, hopefully, do some research on his own to find truth. She was excited to have the opportunity to defend the Christian faith. The following is an excerpt from two of their email dialogues. (Permission from Monica's friend was granted to share his part of her story.)

> **Monica's Story.** So I have some more questions about Mormonism: 1) Are God, Jesus and the Holy Ghost separate gods? Cuz, I was confused by your answer. You said it's not polytheism, but they're still separate. And 2) In Mormonism, how do you have eternal life?

Mormon friend's reply: As for eternal life, let me explain what we know to be the plan of salvation: Before we were born, we lived with our Father in Heaven, as spirits in what is known as the pre-existence. We reached the point where we could no longer progress without receiving bodies and this earthly experience. (Heavenly Father also has a body of flesh and bone.) Heavenly Father presented a plan in which we received bodies, came on earth to live, and had to live by faith. A veil was placed over our minds, so we could not remember the pre-existence while on earth. We would have agency to choose between right and wrong, thereby testing us to see whether or not we would follow our Father in Heaven, who provided the atonement through our elder brother, Jesus Christ, in order to make it possible for us to escape death and sin and return to live with him.

Satan proposed an alternative plan which would deny us of our agency and was cast down, taking one third of all the hosts of heaven with him.

You and I, and all those here on earth, chose to follow Heavenly Father and the Savior.

Now we're here on Earth. When we die, our spirits will separate from our bodies and we will go to the spirit world to await the final judgment. It is in this Spirit World that all those who never had the opportunity to hear the gospel in the flesh will be taught and given the opportunity to accept it. All people who have ever lived will be resurrected and then judged. At the judgment, all of Heavenly Father's children will be judged and separated into three kingdoms of glory.

Satan and his followers (and a select few) will be banished and not receive a kingdom of glory.

Monica's response: Just so you know: I believe that God, the Holy Spirit and Jesus are separate, but they, together, are God, singular. They are separate persons, but they are not separate gods. (Isaiah 43:10, 44:6, 44:8, 45:5-6, 45:18, and 45:21). God keeps saying there are no other gods besides Him, so, therefore, He is the only one. He, God, the great I Am, is the Father, Son, and Holy Spirit. They are referred to as the great I Am. In the New Testament John 8:24, Jesus says that if you don't believe He is the I Am, you will die in your sins. About the pre-existence thing, where is that in the Bible? Where are the three kingdoms found in the Bible?

It is sad to see so many well-meaning, loving people like Monica's friend get pulled into a cult or a pseudo-Christian religion. To answer her final questions, neither the pre-existence thing nor the three kingdoms are found in the Bible. They are, however, very much a part of the Mormon belief system. I have always found it interesting that a lie always takes many words to try to justify itself. For example, the Mormon belief in the Celestial Kingdom essentially says that after you die you will be given a second chance to come to their "Jesus." Scripture (Hebrews 9:27) says it plain and simple: "…man is destined to die once, and after that to face judgment".

How could any thinking person believe in such things that cannot be proven by Scripture or solid historical data? In Agusta's case, she was unhappy and desperate for some kind of hope, and then the Mormons knocked at her door. Although initially, they did not tell her the truth of the Mormon religion, she became attracted to it because of the messengers … those who came to see her. The true goal of a Mormon is to become a god, while the goal of the Christian is to become a willing servant to God and to others. A god or a servant? Thinking that there was really such a choice, which there isn't, many choose becoming a god. Why? So they can be worshiped and rule over others, which is the same desire of Satan. Sadly enough for these people, someday, some dreadful day, they will stand before the One True God and realize, when it is too late, that they have worshiped a false god and now they will be separated forever from God, the One True God (Matthew 25:46, Matthew 7, John 8, Luke 16).

At first glance, Mormonism, like so many other cults, seems appealing. They are pro-family, appear to be good people who do not smoke nor condone taking drugs. It is not until we take a closer, more intimate look below the surface of this cult, that we see the misguided beliefs and practices that exist. When we do learn more about characteristics of these cults, and hear the stories of those who have come out of them, we may mistakenly believe, "That will never happen to me."

But Scripture issues us a very clear warning: "Be self-controlled and alert. Your enemy, the devil, prowls around like a roaring lion looking for someone to devour" (1 Peter 5:8). There are millions of people in the United States and around the world who have fallen prey to the lure of Satan's deception. "Satan himself masquerades as an angel of light" (2 Corinthians 11:14).

All the more reason for Christians to be light to those living in darkness. We must be loving to them, as well as being willing to speak truth. God's Word serves as the plumb line by which all other ideas, prophecies and philosophies must be measured. As we set our hearts on "the way of truth," we will be able to discern the path God has set before us and help others do the same (Psalm 119:30, 105). :: :: ::

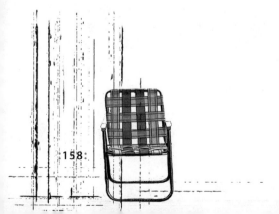

HOW COULD GOD? ::

chapter 12

several years ago, my friend, Cookie, and I were going to play in a golf tournament in Florida. We had not seen much of each other for a long time and were looking forward to catching up. The flight was packed. We found our way to our row and to our pleasant surprise, it was empty, which was a very good thing! I slid over to the window seat and Cookie took the aisle, leaving the middle seat vacant. We could not get over our good fortune. The flight attendant announced that the main door would soon be closed and to hurry and get settled, so we could take off. "Isn't it just like God to give us such a wonderful gift to sit in a row with just two of us! God is good," I said. At that moment, the last passenger stumbled on the plane. It didn't take long for everyone to realize that this guy had way too much to drink. He weaved his way down the aisle and paused by our row. "You're in my seat," he exclaimed. "Move!"

"Lord," I whispered to myself as I was exiting my seat, "I hope you don't mind if I take back that last little bit of thanksgiving I sent to you a few minutes ago."

Our new seatmate, Jim, literally fell into the window seat, leaving a waft of whiskey behind him. I took one look at Cookie and knew that she was not going to give up her aisle seat, so I settled into the dreaded claustrophobic middle position. Soon we were off, and Cookie and I began sharing what God was doing in our ministries and in our lives. For several minutes, Cookie and I were completely immersed in our conversation. Unexpectantly, Jim tapped my shoulder and said, "Can you help me?" "Excuse me," I said, somewhat annoyed to be taken away from my time with Cookie, "What do you mean, 'Can I help you?' I was expecting something cynical, and was wondering what on earth I was going to do, being wedged in my seat on a packed plane, with no place to move. I soon realized that this was no laughing matter as his voice wavered and tears began to flow. "My name is Jim. I have been listening to you and your friend. Maybe you can help me." "What is troubling you?" I said, as I turned toward Jim, no longer aware of the smell of alcohol or the awkwardness of the situation.

"Yesterday, I got a phone call that my son dove into a pool and broke his neck. He's now paralyzed." He started to openly weep. "I don't know what to do. I don't know what to say to my son. Can you please help me?"

I quickly began asking God to please give me the words that he needed to hear. "I am sorry, but I cannot help you. I can't give you the peace that you need, nor can I give you the strength and the words that you need to communicate with your son. However, I do know someone who can help you."

"Who is it?" he asked expectantly.

"This may sound a bit silly to you, but His name is Jesus. You need help from the Great Physician, the One who created the world and all that is in it. He is the only One who can give you the wisdom and peace that you are looking for. He will work through all that you are faced with today and in the days to come. Please know and believe that God loves you and God loves your son. He knows you both by name. He wants to walk through this with you and your son. He wants to bless you in ways you have never dreamed."

We talked for some time. I learned a lot about his family, where he lived and worked. He was a truly nice guy who was absolutely overcome with fear and grief, and his way of dealing with the pain was by drinking. Jim had gone to church and had some knowledge of God, but had never considered God to be personal and forgiving and loving. Jim was soaking up all I had to share with him. He had many questions, and we talked through most of them.

When I travel, I like to carry a small paperback New Testament Bible with me, in case God arranges for an appointment with someone who needs some encouragement. I reached into my carry-on, pulled it out and turned to the book of John. We talked about Jesus being the Word and always being God. I shared with him God's love for all mankind, and His promise that whoever believes in Him will not perish, but will have everlasting life with God in heaven! (John 3:16). I talked about the faithfulness of God and His promise never to leave him.

"God will never force himself into someone's life. You must invite Him in."

"I'm ready to ask Him," Jim said, before I had a chance to finish the sentence.

"Do you believe all that I have told you about God and the Bible?"

"Absolutely," responded Jim.

"Let's pray together," I said, as I took hold of his hand. "I will pray and then you can quietly repeat it after me. OK?"

"I'm ready," said Jim in his loud voice, as he began to sob. I knew he was.

I began to pray quietly with him, and he repeated, with sobs growing louder and louder. Our area of the plane became extremely quiet. (Only God knows who else was praying along!) We continued praying and I thanked God for arranging this moment with Him. Jim affirmed that he believed in Jesus, and invited Him to come into his life. He repeated the prayer with words and with his heart.

Jim became a believer that day. His situation had not changed, but he had. He was still flying to Florida to see his son who would, most likely, never walk again. Now, by the grace of God, Jim had hope and the outward appearance, and certainly the inward confirmation, of peace. He promised that he would read the book of John at least three times and talk to some of his Christian friends about the commitment that he had made that day. He put the Bible in his shirt pocket and said, "I can't wait to tell my son about this! We have so much to talk about!" The plane landed and Jim couldn't wait to get on his way. I gave him a hug and off he went to be with his son.

Oh yes, about Cookie. She was a mess; she had been crying right along with Jim. She prayed for both of us while we were talking. I thank God for her support! As we were deplaning, I had some business to attend to with a friend of mine. "Lord, about my taking back my thank you for the empty seat … Thank You, Lord, for using me in spite of my selfish self. You are a most loving and merciful God. Please be with Jim, his son and his family as he continues on his difficult journey. Thanks."

We have all experienced suffering. Some is catastrophic, and other is less life-changing. One moment all is well, and in an instant, the horror of the brevity of life is looking at us in the face. An earthquake, a tsunami, war, disease, accident, divorce, betrayal … Where are You, God? How could You, a loving God, allow such things to happen? I can't help but doubt You. Can You hear me? Where are You, God, in the midst of all this pain and suffering?

The problem of suffering is perhaps the most difficult challenge a believer will face, in regards to their belief in the God of the Bible. Scripture teaches that

God is all-powerful (omnipotent) and all-loving (omni-benevolent). The question that often arises in the mind and heart of the believer and unbeliever, alike, is: If God is all-powerful and all-loving, and could stop anything that is impeding our happiness and health, why does He allow it? Does He want us to suffer? Why, God, why?

In working through these questions, it is essential to see what the Bible has to say about the suffering. We can learn much if we go to the beginning of the Bible, to the book of Genesis. "In the beginning God created the heavens and the earth" (Genesis 1:1). In Genesis 1:3-25 God tells us the order of His creation and that it was all "good." In Genesis 1:26, God made male and female in His image and said in verse 31 that it was "very good." The two people that God created, Adam and Eve, lived in the Garden of Eden. All was well. Adam and Eve walked with God and communicated directly with Him. There was no suffering or death. It was like heaven on earth. So what happened?

God did not create robots. He created humans in His image, so that God could love them and they in turn can love Him. He wanted to have fellowship with them, bless and give all mankind life to the full. God wants to call us friend. True love, God's love, requires choice. God chose to first love mankind, but did not force mankind to love Him in return. In Genesis 2:16-17, God introduced Adam to choice and the consequences of bad choices, when God told him that "You are free to eat from any tree in the garden; but you must not eat from the tree of the knowledge of good and evil, for when you eat of it you will surely die." For the first time in Adam's life, he had to choose between right and wrong, good and evil, God or self. Was he going to obey or disobey God? With choice comes free will.

In Genesis 3:1-6, Satan, the serpent, introduces himself to Adam and Eve and immediately plants a seed of doubt by saying, "Did God really say...?" This is how Satan works; he plants doubt, and will always misrepresent the truth of God. Here we see Satan informing Adam and Eve that God would not judge them to death for their disobedience. Satan also lies about the very nature of our merciful and generous God, by insinuating that God withholds from Adam and Eve (and future mankind) those things that are beneficial and make them feel good. First Eve, and then Adam, disobeyed God and believed Satan, the serpent. At that moment, the first sin was committed and fellowship was broken between God and mankind. Adam then began the spiritual and physical death that God had warned them about. Adam did not fall over dead, but began the dying process that continued to the physical end of his life.

"Therefore, just as sin entered the world through one man, and death through sin, and in this way death came to all men, because all sinned" (Romans 5:12).

Before we think that God was too harsh in His judgment, note that in Genesis 3:15 God provides hope. It is the first prophecy, telling us of the Messiah that would come and take away the penalty of the sin of the world by dying for us! Until then, God handed out consequences for the sin that was committed. For the woman, it was pain in childbearing (Genesis 3:16-17). For the man, he will painfully work all the days of his life. The ground will produce thorns and thistles and man will eat from the plants of the field (Genesis 3:17-19).

As a result of sin, we, as humans, become sinners both by nature and by choice. If we can read a newspaper or watch television, we know that mankind is very capable of doing evil things to one another, which bring about much suffering. C.S. Lewis, author of "The Problem of Pain," estimates that 80 percent of all pain is caused by human agents.[1] We do great damage to one another: physically, mentally, emotionally and spiritually. Nothing personal, but all of us, by nature, are incredibly selfish, and want things to go our way. When they don't, we often react in ways that are not honoring to God. We hate it when this happens, but before we know what happened, we do it again! Paul had the same issues.

Romans 7:15-20 (The Apostle Paul speaking) "I do not understand what I do. For what I want to do, I do not do, but what I hate, I do. And if I do what I do not want to do, I agree that the law is good. As it is, it is no longer I myself who do it, but it is sin living in me. I know that nothing good lives in me, that is, in my sinful nature. For I have the desire to do what is good, but I cannot carry it out. For what I do is not the good I want to do; no, the evil I do not want to do—this I keep on doing. Now if I do what I do not want to do, it is no longer I who do it, but it is sin living in me that does it"

Romans 7:24-25 (The Apostle Paul speaking) "What a wretched man I am! Who will rescue me from this body of death? Thanks be to God—through Jesus Christ our Lord!"

What about our response to things that happen to us that are out of our control? What about dealing with the death of a sibling?

Katie's Story. Death has been something with which I have become painfully familiar. Perhaps not in the eyes of the one who has lost every family member in a war, or all their children in a car accident, but to me it never feels far away.

The first person I remember dying was my grandfather, my mother's father. I was nine. I remember his funeral. I remember my mom's tears, and those of so many others. I remember my tears as I sat in the pew knowing my grandfather's body would be spread over a lake. I remember asking about heaven, while continually searching for hope. One year later, I would find that the hope I searched for would only be found in a relationship with Jesus Christ.

Following the loss of my grandpa, my sophomore year of high school, a friend died in a car accident after five days in a coma. Junior year, one of my best friend's brothers died of cancer. Senior year, a good friend's mom died of cancer. Freshman year of college, my great grandmother died. Senior year of college, there were two striking deaths: one, a friend from high school and college died in Afghanistan, and two weeks later, my sister died of cancer.

Those are the facts. I share that with you so that you will know my acquaintance with suffering—not just my own, but that of other's, too. Suffering shows itself different in everyone, and at every funeral, despite the traditional hymns and Scripture, there is either hope or there isn't. I came to know the Lord when I was 10. I knew "what it took" to get to heaven, and that outside of Jesus, there is no hope. This is the reason I have survived the suffering, the thoughts, the fears; because at the end of the day, God is hope. Jesus died so that we might not only have life here, on earth, but in heaven as well.

Two weeks before my sister died, I went to the funeral of my friend who died in Afghanistan. I have never seen people, despite true suffering and questions as to "Why now?" filled with such hope. I have never known a bigger celebration of life. Because of Brett's relationship with Jesus, we had, not only hope, but assurance that He had now entered into God's eternal and glorious kingdom.

God can allow suffering because it brings us closer to Him. This is His ultimate goal. He does not desire for you to hurt or suffer. He does not desire for you to be in pain. What He does desire is for you to know the all-surpassing greatness of His love, and that that is what will get you through this life.

My sister had cancer. It had developed out of a disease she had from the time she was three months old. She was 25 when she was diagnosed, and nine months later, God called her home. There was a malignant tumor in her leg, and the cancer had spread to her brain, lungs and neck. She had surgeries, chemotherapy and radiation. Nothing was getting better. In the matter of a few weeks, we went from knowing we had less than a year with her, to 24 hours. The shock of knowing someone you have known since the day you were born, and in my case 21 years, was no longer going to be with you, raises questions. But given that we had less than 24 hours, there was no time to question. The time we spent with Sarah in her hospital room the last 24 hours of her life was precious. It was filled with so many people, prayers, songs, and, at the end, we sang her into heaven. We were not able to do this because we were "super Christians," or because people were watching and our reputations were at stake; but we were able to let Jesus take her home because of God's presence in that room, because of the hope to which He had called us.

My sister was a follower of Jesus. She knew Jesus in the most precious of ways. Throughout her fight with cancer, we knew God could heal her. But we also knew if He chose to take her home, if He saw that she had completed what He set before her on this earth, that that would have to be ok, and that that was His will. We chose to remember that God's will is good, pleasing and perfect. Yes, we suffer, but that is neither the goal, nor the end. As the day approaches, being two years from the time when I have heard her voice, seen her smile or felt her touch, it is with joy that I can say she is in heaven. Sarah's "death" was not about my suffering, but rather, it was about God relieving her of her suffering. Her life on earth was by no means easy. Her physical, emotional and social pain I cannot grasp, nor do I dare to. But on April 10, 2005, God, in His grace, decided to end that pain. And by that same grace we live on, in the hope that we will yet dance with her on the streets of gold.

Though suffering is ultimately caused by sin, is the end result always evil?

No. In the case of Katie's sister, her suffering resulted in her being in heaven because of her faith in Jesus Christ. There she no longer suffers. She has no pain, no tears, and will live forever with Jesus. The truth of the matter is, if she had a choice to come back to earth healthy or stay in heaven, she would stay in heaven. In our wildest imagination we have no idea how incredibly awesome heaven is until we get there!

Sometimes God wants to take us away from our pain. For others, suffering is a wake-up call from God. Some of us live ignoring God, and suffering oftentimes forces us to look for answers outside of ourselves.

> "Pain insists upon being attended to. God whispers to us in our pleasures, speaks in our conscience, and shouts in our pain. It is His megaphone to rouse a deaf world." – **C.S. Lewis**[3]

Today, we tend to take sin lightly, thinking that it is not a big deal, because everyone does it. Don't underestimate the devastation and power that sin has in our lives. Sin is a terrible thing! It not only brought about death and the curse on all of mankind, but also, because of its terribleness, corrupted Creation itself. It is the source of all death and suffering that comes through the natural order like disease, tornadoes and other natural disasters (Romans 8:20-22).

God desires for all of mankind to repent and come into a personal relationship with Him, ultimately entering into God's kingdom—to return to the life God intended from the beginning. "… that the eyes of your heart may be enlightened in order that you may know the hope to which he has called you, the riches of his glorious inheritance in the saints" (Ephesians 1:18).

What are the riches of His glorious inheritance? Read Ephesians 1 and drink in all that the Lord has done. Among many things, He has chosen us to be holy and blameless in His sight (Ephesians 1:4). Being holy, set apart from the world, is not something that comes naturally to us. Being set apart from the world and leading lives that are pleasing to God are not goals that we easily set for ourselves because living that sort of life is hard. Most of us desire for life to be easy, but God did not call us to an easy life!

Isaiah 53:1-12 Who has believed our message and to whom has the arm of the LORD been revealed? He grew up before him like a tender shoot, and like a root out of dry ground. He had no beauty or majesty to attract us to him, nothing in his appearance that we should desire him. He was despised and rejected by men, a man of sorrows, and familiar with suffering. Like one from whom men hide their faces he was despised, and we esteemed him not. Surely he took up our infirmities and carried our sorrows, yet we considered him stricken by God, smitten by him, and afflicted. But he was pierced for our transgressions, he was crushed for our iniquities; the punishment that brought us peace was upon him, and by his wounds we are healed. We all, like sheep, have gone astray, each of us has turned to his own way; and the LORD has laid on him the iniquity of us all.

He was oppressed and afflicted, yet he did not open his mouth; he was led like a lamb to the slaughter, and as a sheep before her shearers is silent, so he did not open his mouth. By oppression and judgment he was taken away. And who can speak of his descendants? For he was cut off from the land of the living; for the transgression of my people he was stricken. He was assigned a grave with the wicked, and with the rich in his death, though he had done no violence, nor was any deceit in his mouth.

Yet it was the LORD'S will to crush him and cause him to suffer, and though the LORD makes his life a guilt offering, he will see his offspring and prolong his days, and the will of the LORD will prosper in his hand. After the suffering of his soul, he will see the light [of life] and be satisfied; by his knowledge my righteous servant will justify many, and he will bear their iniquities. Therefore I will give him a portion among the great, and he will divide the spoils with the strong, because he poured out his life unto death, and was numbered with the transgressors. He bore the sin of many, and made intercession for the transgressors.

When I read these passages I cannot, in my wildest dreams, imagine why God did this for us. Even if we all fell down in overwhelming thanksgiving to Him for the life Christ led here on earth and what He did for all mankind on the cross, I still don't get it. Even if we all led lives that daily, moment by moment, gave Him glory, the question remains: Why would Jesus do such a thing? Knowing how the Church treats Him today, I have no idea why He doesn't blow us all into some eternal fire!

When it comes to suffering, my question to God is not "Why, God, have you allowed this to happen to me?" but rather, "Why not me?" I have come to the conclusion that this whole idea of suffering is often thought of with faulty expectations as to how we think our lives should be lived. Most all of us would expect to be healthy in body, mind and spirit. I used to expect, and even think that it was due me, to have plenty of clothes to wear and food to eat, to drive a car, live in a house, have a husband who loved me as Christ loves the Church along with perfect children. I thought this was how life should be, not only for myself, but for my friends and family. Interestingly enough, God has a broader and deeper purpose for our lives!

Karen's Story. I often wondered why Paul wrote that we should have joy in the midst of our trials. In my study of the Minor Prophets the summer before my senior year of college, I found my answer. In both Nehemiah and Jeremiah it says, "The Joy of the Lord is our strength."

My junior year of college, I did an internship with a well known company for my accounting degree. I had the hardest semesters of my life. The spiritual warfare was immensely intense that semester and I was so broken and humbled by the trial! Nancy found the semester somewhat relieving, as I think she thought things came too easily for me, and that my faith needed to be tried and tested—and it was tried and tested. Without going into details, suffice it to say that I was refined that semester—and I felt the heat! After that semester, I told God that I didn't care what He asked me to do, I would go to a foreign country, I would work for next to nothing, but I did not want a job in public accounting!

God says in Isaiah 55, "My thoughts are not your thoughts, neither are your ways my ways." God had plans for me that were much more His ways than mine. Through a series of circumstances, I was offered a job during my senior year of college to work at a public accounting firm. My stomach churned! But after much prayer, I knew that God was leading me to this job. I told God that I would not be Jonah. I would go apprehensively, but obediently. While God continues to unveil facets of His character, I knew Him well enough to know that He would get me there one way or another; and given the choice, I preferred to go on my own free will, not in the belly of a whale. I accepted my job in October, and hoped that this was "my Isaac"—that God was testing my obedience and that He would see that I was willing to lay my plan on the altar. How I prayed that God would provide a ram, and provide another way; but God determined my calling was to be in public accounting.

I spent close to the next three years trying to pass the Certified Public Accounting exam. It became evidently clear to me that God's timing is perfect. It rarely is what I wish it to be, but He is never late. So, I would wait until He determined that it was His time for me to pass the exam. Not long after passing, I transitioned to another position in the firm, which is a much better fit for my personality and gifts. Without the experience that I had, or the timing of when this occurred, I probably would never have been given the opportunity of this position, nor would I have recognized this job for the true gift that it is. It is one absolutely apparent blessing that I see from that whole experience, and I frequently thank God for the richness of the job I currently have. I am sure that there are other unknown reasons for my three years of waiting, as well, but only time will tell!

Why shouldn't we suffer? We live in a world that is broken, that is inhabited with broken, selfish people. Suffering, whether we like it or not, is part of life on this earth. That is why God tells us that He will be there for us when we do suffer (James 11:33). Hopefully, that suffering will drive us to restoration and healing that could only come from God. God promises that all things will work together for good for those who trust God. Check out the next verse, it holds the key to the purpose of suffering.

Romans 8:28-30 And we know that in all things, God works for the good of those who love him, who have been called according to his purpose. For those God foreknew he also predestined to be conformed to the likeness of his Son, that he might be the firstborn among many brothers.

Our purpose in life is to be conformed to the likeness of His Son. How does that happen for us? It happens through blessings and through suffering. Both are gifts from God and, as a result of these things, we are changed to bring Him glory.

Maybe suffering is not the curse that we have thought it to be. I am not diminishing the deep crushing pain of losing someone or something. I know what that feels like. I also know that, through it all, I am being drawn closer to God, if I allow Him to teach me amidst the pain. I am better for it!

There is suffering to be expected if we are walking obediently in the footsteps of Christ. Look at what Christ went through. It should not surprise us that a multitude of things go sideways when we are living out the Christian worldview. When I am being attacked because of who I am in Christ, or by those who hate what I am doing with my life, it is confirmation that I am doing what God called me to do, because Satan would not be attacking if I were not following Him!

2 Timothy 3:12 In fact, everyone who wants to live a godly life in Christ Jesus will be persecuted.

James 1:2-4 Consider it pure joy, my brothers, whenever you face trials of many kinds, because you know that the testing of your faith develops perseverance. Perseverance must finish its work so that you may be mature and complete, not lacking anything.

There will be a day when there will be no more pain, suffering, persecuting or death! (Revelation 21, Isaiah 11, 2 Peter 3). In the meantime, we will all suffer from our own sin, the sin of others, or our sin condition from birth. Know that through it all, there is Jesus, calling to us to come to Him so that He can give us the comfort and direction that we need. There is a reason for all of it. Our hope comes from the One who suffered and died in our place, to pay for the penalty of our sin. Jesus is the only true answer to the problem of suffering. Remember, in the midst of our suffering, there is a God, the great I AM.

I want to share with you parts of a talk that Coach Tony Dungy spoke at a breakfast for Athletes in Action before the 2006 Super Bowl. I hope that what Coach Dungy had to say about suffering will help shed some light on this issue and will give you peace as well.

Tony spoke about his son, Jordan, who was born with a neurological condition that does not allow him to feel any pain. It sounds like a good thing not to feel pain, but the consequences of such a condition can be very dangerous. "We've learned a lot about pain in the last five years we've had Jordan. We've learned some hurts are really necessary for kids. Pain is necessary for kids to find out the difference between what's good and what's harmful. Cookies are good, but in Jordan's mind, if they're good out on the plate, they're even better in the oven. He will go right in the oven when my wife's not looking, reach in, take the rack out, take the pan out, burn his hands and eat the cookies and burn his tongue and never feel it. He doesn't know that's bad for him. Jordan has no fear of anything, so we constantly have to watch him.

"You get the question all the time, 'Why does the Lord allow pain in your life? Why do bad things happen to good people? If God is a God of love, why does He allow these hurtful things to happen?'"

"We've learned that a lot of times, because of that pain, that little temporary pain, you learn what's harmful. You learn to fear the right things. Pain sometimes lets us know we have a condition that needs to be healed. Pain inside sometimes lets us know that spiritually we're not quite right, and we need to be healed and that God will send that healing agent right to the spot. Sometimes, pain is the only way that will turn us as kids back to the Father."

James Dungy, Tony's oldest son, died three days before Christmas. He spoke of the suffering and what he learned through this experience. "It was tough, and it was very, very painful, but as painful as it was, there were some good things that came out of it." He spoke of how he wished that he would have given his son a big hug before he left home for the last time. "I met a guy the next day after the funeral," Tony said. "He said, 'I was there. I heard you talking. I took off work today. I called my son. I told him I was taking him to the movies. We're going to spend some time and go to dinner.' That was a real, real blessing to me.

"We got a letter back two weeks ago that two people had received his corneas, and now they can see. That's been a tremendous blessing." Tony also said he received a letter from a girl from the family's church in Tampa. She had known James for many years. She went to the funeral because she knew James. "When I saw what happened at the funeral, and your family and the celebration and how it was handled, that was the first time I realized there had to be a God. I accepted Christ into my life and my life's been different since that day."

"That was an awesome blessing, so all of those things kind of made me realize what God's love is all about."

"People asked me, 'How did you recover so quickly?' I'm not totally recovered. I don't know that I ever will be. Because of Christ's spirit in me, I have the peace of mind in the midst of something that's very, very painful. That's my prayer today, that everyone in this room would know the same thing."

Tony Dungy knows his God and understands the bigger picture of life and suffering. Through his witness here in Indianapolis, many lives have been changed … including my own.

In the midst of suffering … I AM. :: :: ::

SO THAT'S WHO YOU ARE!::

chapter 13

a.w. tozer, the popular 20th century author and pastor, asks this question: "What comes into your mind when you think about God?" Good question! For as he explains, "What comes into our minds when we think about God is the most important thing about us."[1] Our understanding of God dictates how we all will live our lives. If God is not a part of your life, you know that you live by your own rules. Even if those rules include being a wonderful friend and doing service to others, you are still ultimately living for yourself. However, when it comes right down to it, a life without God in the center is a life without hope, purpose and ultimate reward.

My question is this: How can I lead a life that is pleasing to God if I don't know Him? Jesus asked the question of us when He said, "Who do people (you) say I am?" (Mark 8:27).

Ask the man or woman on the street and you will get answers that range from one end of the spectrum to another. "He is good and loving" to "He is vengeful and full of anger." Others say, "He doesn't exist," or "I don't know if He exists." The pantheists would say that God is in everything and everybody. The list of responses is endless. All of these responses cannot be true. Is there a God? If so, is it possible to know Him?

As we have seen, everyone seems to have an opinion as to who God is or is not. Our opinions and biases come primarily from our personal life experiences. As I mentioned previously, my childhood perception of God was that He was a God who was distant, cold and, frankly, scary. For someone who was abused as a child, they might see God as someone who did not care, was absent or nonexistent. Someone growing up with an unloving and emotionally absent father might not be able to see God as his Father without shuddering. On the other hand, there are those who have had lives with loving fathers and mothers, relatively stress free, who believe without much thought. Then there are those who have been through extreme stress, hurt and pain from their personal life circumstances, so God is all they have in life that offers hope and life. How do you see Him? Why?

Some experiences direct us to the God of Scriptures, and others mislead us into thinking that God is something that He is not. Emotional responses to our circumstances are real, and paint very vivid pictures in our minds that dictate how we see life, situations, people and, yes, God. Learning to see God as He really is oftentimes involves as much unlearning as it does learning. This is why it is so important for Christians to live out our faith, so that others can see God by the way we treat others, as well as being able to give the reason for the hope that we have in Jesus with much gentleness and respect. Rocky is one that had a lot of unlearning to do in his journey to find a Father who would never leave or forsake him.

> **Rocky's Story.** I am of Jewish and Italian descent and was born in 1985. I remember celebrating a little Chanukah and Christmas, but not really thinking much of either, except all the presents, to be quite honest. When I was about seven, my mother, now a beautiful woman of God, was struggling greatly as God was in the process of growing, maturing and healing her wounds from her childhood. My father was ill at the time and I didn't get to see him. I was put in a children's home. Though I was only there a few months, it seemed like years. I felt alone, lost and confused as to who I was and most certainly who God was. It was a very dark time for me. My older sister came and got me and took custody of me, along with the man who would soon become her husband. They provided a home for me and my sister continually reminded me that there was a God who loved me and would take care of me. I knew there was a God, but I didn't know much about Him.
>
> When I was about 15 years old, I went to live with my brother and had a great experience at school. I excelled in grades and at track, but with more success, the emptier I felt. I had the unhealthy fear of God and was worried about what would happen when I died. I had to find out for myself who this God really was. When I finally began to seek the truth, I found that the God of the Jews is the same God who promised He would come in the flesh. I, not having a biological earthly father for long, desperately wanted to better understand the character of God. I found that God was who He said He was, as I began to study the Scriptures.
>
> God showed His faithfulness to me by sending to me a woman named Kim, and her son, Tommy, who unofficially adopted me. They were strong Christians and lived their lives in a way that dripped of love, understanding and forgiveness. It was through them that I, for the first

time, began to see God as the Father that I never had. The more I learned about Him, the more secure I felt and for the first time, I could rest at night knowing that if I died, I would, for sure, spend eternity with God. My family is pretty mixed. We all have different last names, but I have learned that it is not the human blood line that is important, but rather, the blood that Christ shed on the cross for me.

Life still has its challenges, but this much I know: God is my Redeemer, my Savior and my Rescuer!

Rocky could have allowed his circumstances to shape his view of the character of his God. God made provisions, though, so that he would have someplace else to learn about Him. Not only did his sister minister truth to him, but He also brought Kim and Tommy into Rocky's life to model the peace and love. His search did not end there, because Rocky also went to the Scriptures to find how God defined Himself. So, who is He? Can I find the One True God in spite of my circumstances and my finite mind? The answer is a resounding "YES!"

We have looked at the Bible and found that it is reliable and true because of the way that the scribes wrote it, by how it compares with other works of antiquity, the fulfilled prophecies, and the writings of men that were living during the time of Jesus, as well as the confirmation found through archaeology. You have read about the resurrection of Jesus and have seen how this event is the most well-documented event in human history. Bottom line: the Bible is true and its contents can be trusted. The death and resurrection of Christ did happen, and because of it we can know with assurance that Jesus is God and that we, as believers, will go to heaven to live forever with God.

How do we know who God really is? With complete assurance we can know who God really is through the Scriptures. God speaks loud and clear for Himself.

:: God is the One True God

Rocky found the One True God of the Scripture is separate from all other gods. He is the One in whom we can put our hope, and no longer have to be deceived by the false gods who bring chaos instead of peace into the world. Isaiah 45:5-6 "I am the LORD, and there is no other; apart from me there is no God. I will strengthen you, though you have not acknowledged me, so that from the rising of the sun to the place of its setting, men may know there is none besides me. I am the LORD, and there is no other." Because God says He is the One True God, He expects us to worship just Him. Know, too, that God is the God over all false gods forever. He can never be replaced because He always was and always will be the great I AM (Revelation 22:13).

:: God Is Good

Psalm 25:8 Good and upright is the LORD; therefore he instructs sinners in his ways.

I can't begin to tell you how many times I have heard someone try their hardest to escape the ultimate issue of salvation by saying, "Well, I am a good person. I haven't killed anyone and I volunteer for a lot of good causes." My first response to that is, how do you know you are good enough? Who do you think sets the standard for good? God, Himself is the embodiment of good. God, Himself is the standard for good, man is not. God is not sometimes good, He is always good because He IS good. He can never do something bad, it is not in His nature. No one can tag an attribute on God, He is the attribute.

In His goodness, sometimes God interrupts our lives with the impossible. Jason Patchett, who is a Christian recording artist, was a student who was surprised by the goodness and mercy of God.

> **Jason's story.** As a senior in high school, I was faced with a decision that was not uncommon to people my age. I had decided that I would apply to a small Christian school to pursue musical studies (early in the spring semester of my senior year). Finally, I had received my acceptance letter and I registered to attend. This seemed like it was God's plan for my life, until He surprised me with other plans. One week before the first payment was due to the college, I was presented with the opportunity to travel to Memphis, Tennessee, to begin work on my first professional recording project.
>
> This decision was a very easy decision to make, and yet at the same time, it was very hard. It was an easy decision because I had always wanted to pursue a ministry in music ever since I was a young boy. It was a difficult decision, however, because I had no idea where this road would lead and if I would be making a mistake by missing my formal education at this point in my life. My family prayed about it and we decided that it was God's will to fulfill a life dream and continue with college as soon as I could. Soon after, I wrote a song called "Steps of Faith," that served as an encouragement to others and myself that God would show us through times that seem like we are blind to the road ahead.

Now, nearly two years later, I have been blessed to experience the power of God through lives being changed through music. God has given me a message that I believe to be the driving force of my ministry. I am still currently ministering through music, and at the same time I am preparing to minister to the youth of the church. God is good. Who but God would allow me to do what I love to do? He broke through the barriers of impossibilities and opened up doors that I would never have dreamed possible.

No doubt, you are probably asking yourself, "If God is so good, then why … ? Please read the chapter "How Could God?" Suffice it to say that there is much that happens to us and to others which makes no sense! It does to God.

Hosea 11:9 For I am God, and not man—the Holy One among you.

Beyond our mind's ability to think or comprehend is God, to whom all things make sense. Someday when we are with Christ in heaven, we will understand. Scripture confirms this in Romans 8:28, "And we know that in all things God works for the good of those who love him, who have been called according to his purpose."

:: God is love

As an agnostic planning our wedding, Ed and I decided that we wanted to have 1 Corinthians 13 read during the ceremony. It was a part of my sorority ritual and it fulfilled the "requirement" of having some Scripture read during the ceremony. It wasn't until years later, as a believer, that I began to understand the significance of these beautiful words.

1 Corinthians 13:1-13 If I speak in the tongues of men and of angels, but have not love, I am only a resounding gong or a clanging cymbal. If I have the gift of prophecy and can fathom all mysteries and all knowledge, and if I have a faith that can move mountains, but have not love, I am nothing. If I give all I possess to the poor and surrender my body to the flames, but have not love, I gain nothing.

Love is patient, love is kind. It does not envy, it does not boast, it is not proud. It is not rude, it is not self-seeking, it is not easily angered, it keeps no record of wrongs. Love does not delight in evil but rejoices with the truth. It always protects, always trusts, always hopes, always perseveres.

Love never fails. But where there are prophecies, they will cease; where there are tongues, they will be stilled; where there is knowledge, it will pass away. For we know in part and we prophesy in part, but when perfection comes, the imperfect disappears. When I was a child, I talked like a child, I thought like a child, I reasoned like a child. When I became a man, I put childish ways behind me. Now we see but a poor reflection as in a mirror; then we shall see face to face. Now I know in part; then I shall know fully, even as I am fully known.

And now these three remain: faith, hope and love. But the greatest of these is love.

God is love. Not some of the time, not in degrees, but full-out unconditional love all the time. God could not love you more, no matter what you do or who you are: a believer in Him or not! Whether or not you want to be loved by God, you are. There is nothing you can do to increase God's love for you, or nothing you can do to diminish God's love toward you. He loves you with an ἀγάπν (agape) love that is eternal, pure and unaltered by condition. God loves you because He is love. Therefore, it is impossible to truly love someone unconditionally, perfectly, unless it is God in you (the Holy Spirit) doing the loving. As real as love might feel or seem to be, unless God is in the mix, it is not true, lifelong, unconditional love.

Take a minute and re-read 1 Corinthians 13, but this time substitute God for the word love.

No wonder the things we try to accomplish in the flesh might work for a time, but often do not last. If we decide we want to do something wonderful for God, but He is not the author and sustainer of the event, be assured that He will not receive the glory. Ever wonder why so many "love" relationships do not work? Again, if God is love, and if He is not at the center of the relationship, the girl cannot love the guy as God intended him to be loved, and neither can the guy love the girl as God has designed.

Any relationship that is worth something must be worked on. Find someone who is happily married and ask if a good marriage takes lots of work. No doubt they will smile and agree wholeheartedly. Any friendship takes work, and so does a vibrant relationship with Christ. We get to know Him as we read the Scriptures and pray. Can you imagine how pleased God is when one of His children takes time out of their busy day to actually sit still, and listen to God speaking to them personally through the Scriptures? The more I am in the Scriptures, the less demanding I am in my own personal requests for fixing things and people, and the more open I become to wanting God's perfect will for my life. Go figure, the Almighty Creator God wants to have a very personal, active, real relationship with you!

James 2:23 And the scripture was fulfilled that says, "Abraham believed God and it was credited to him as righteousness," and he was called God's friend.

:: God is unchanging

Another astounding truth about God is that, unlike us, He never changes. How often do we vary in how we feel toward someone? How many times do we do something that is good one minute, and then turn around and do something that is hurtful the next? God does not have that problem because He is immutable; He never changes. He is who He is.

James 1:17 Every good and perfect gift comes from above, coming down from the Father of the heavenly lights, who does not change like shifting shadows.

The good news in this is that God is always good and loving, because He is good and loving. He can never stop being who He is. Whatever it is that appears to us as God being anything less than good and loving, cannot be true. Because I cannot figure something out does not give me the right to assume that God is anything less than good and loving. Because God is unchanging, I know that He will never stop loving me or being good to me. This truth gives me much peace as I live each day in a world that is constantly changing.

:: God is all-present

From the Scriptures we learn about the omnipresence of God. He is "all-present," which means He is not limited to space or time. God exists everywhere at all times, and cannot be contained by any one or anything.

Jeremiah 23:23-24 "Am I only a God nearby," declares the LORD, "and not a God far away? Can anyone hide in secret places so that I cannot see him?" declares the LORD. "Do I not fill heaven and earth?" declares the LORD.

Don't confuse this attribute of God to be pantheistic in nature. The pantheists believe that God is in everything. The Christian believes that God is separate from His creation, but is present everywhere at all times. There are no random molecules … nothing that is beyond God's presence.

I remember playing hide and seek with my kids when they were young, and their idea of hiding was to put their hands over their eyes and tell me to try to find them. We laugh, but we probably all did it as we were growing up, because our understanding of life was very limited at that young age. I imagine that God looks upon those of you who are trying to hide from Him with a bit of a smile on His face, as well. There is no secret place from God, either outside or inside your being.

As spring prom time approaches, I invariably get a call from a parent asking me to speak to the students about what not to do on prom night. They should be concerned, as the highest birth rates for teens are nine months after prom. My talk with the students lasts a minute or two, as I review the omnipresence of God!

:: God is all-knowing

God is also omniscient, all-knowing. Can you imagine a God who knows everything that has ever happened and everything that will ever happen? God is never surprised.

Psalm 139:2-4 You know when I sit and when I rise; you perceive my thoughts from afar. You discern my going out and my lying down; you are familiar with all my ways. Before a word is on my tongue you know it completely, O LORD.

And to think that He loves us anyway!

If I had understood the omniscience of God, I would not have been so surprised to learn about the hundreds of prophecies in Scripture that came true hundreds of years after they were predicted by prophets in the Old Testament. That is why I can say with confidence that when I die, I am going to heaven. Not because I am living a perfect life, because I am not. I know that I am going to heaven because God spoke it in the Scriptures (John 3:16) and because God is the One True God who is always loving, good, true, immutable and all-knowing, who would never promise something that He was not going to bring to fruition. This is why Scripture says, "… that he who began a good work in you will carry it on to completion until the day of Christ Jesus" (Philippians 1:6).

If God knows everything, then why do we pray? When Jesus was in the Garden of Gethsemane, He prayed to the Father about what was about to happen to Him. Jesus knew from the beginning of time that He would suffer a gruesome death on the cross for the sole purpose of paying the penalty of the sins of the world.

Romans 6:23 For the wages of sin is death, but the gift of God is eternal life in Christ Jesus our Lord.

He was well aware of what this experience was going to be like, including, for the first and last time from eternity past to eternity future, a momentary separation from the Father. Only when we get to heaven will we ever be able to understand fully the price of the sacrifice that Jesus made for all of us on the cross.

Luke 22:41-44 (Jesus praying) "He withdrew about a stone's throw beyond them, knelt down and prayed, 'Father, if you are willing, take this cup from me; yet not my will, but yours be done.' An angel from heaven appeared to him and strengthened him. And being in anguish, he prayed more earnestly, and his sweat was like drops of blood falling to the ground."

Do you see it? "Not my will, but Yours be done." Could it be that when we pray, God wants us to not only praise Him and thank Him for who He is and all that He has done, but also to seek His will, not our own, for our lives? Prayer is time for God to make His requests known to us as much, if not more, as it is for us to make ours known to Him. How often do we rip through our check lists, sign off and call it prayer, with no intention of listening to God speak to us through His love letter, the Scriptures?

:: God is faithful
If God knows all about us, and sees us at our worst, why does He stick with us? The Bible says that God is faithful, merciful and full of grace. He loves us. That's why, period! God can always be depended on to do what He says. Even when we don't deserve God's love, He is faithful to love us anyway!

2 Timothy 2:13 ... if we are faithless, He will remain faithful, for He cannot disown himself.

If it were possible to use words to tell of the very nature of God, we would run out of paper and time before the list would be complete. As God is eternal, so are the attributes of His nature. We can talk about His Holiness, His mercy, His righteousness, His truthfulness, His forgiveness, His perfection and His greatness, but the essence of all that is said and written is that whatever it is about God, it is beyond our human understanding! He is who He says He is all of the time. Nothing can, nor will ever, change that. The purity and magnitude of each of the attributes of God we cannot begin to fathom with our finite minds. Because the Holy Spirit lives in me, I am able to know Him in ways I could not have comprehended before I believed that Jesus was the Savior.

God is not limited by anything. If He were, He would cease to be God, and that is what separates Him from all other "gods." All other gods are limited in some way, because they are nothing more than man's invention. When we downsize God, we fail to let Him be who He is … the beginning and the end, the Alpha and the Omega.

If we Christians are to promote truth to our culture and live out the Christian worldview with confidence, it is a necessity that we know who God is, despite what our feelings may tell us. God's Word holds the key in promoting a clear picture of the one true God.

As we begin to understand who God really is, what is our response? How does it affect our very being? How does it affect the way we live our lives? The more we know of God, the more it should cultivate within us a heart of thankfulness and trust, as well as a willing submission to the lordship of Christ.

Are there areas of your life you need to give over to God? Are you willing to do it? In submitting yourself completely to His will, you will find greater joy and freedom than you have ever known. We can give up control of our lives, because there is One—the perfect, loving God—who can oversee our lives better than we ever could.

Are you ready to completely trust your God? He is waiting for you to take that step. :: :: ::

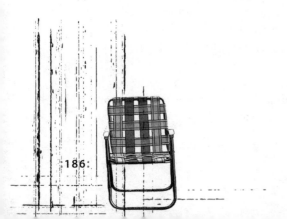

LIVE IT!::

chapter 14

:: What God?

it takes time to learn it and boldness to speak it, but to live out the Christian worldview, that's another thing. What does it look like to live out our faith? Can it really be done?

We are torn between choosing to live our lives the way that God designed them to be lived, versus being pulled by the world that encourages the quick fix and instant gratification. It is a continual battle, because we are imperfect and often weak people, living in a world that promises to satisfy our every need without God. Most of us are pretty good at spiritualizing our reasons for choosing our own way over God's best for us. We are people who think that we can do it better and quicker ourselves, and being naturally selfish, living God's way is difficult—but without Him, it is impossible.

I am reminded of a time that I, as a new believer in Jesus, was playing in the final match of a golf tournament that brought out a good sized crowd of spectators. At this point in my spiritual journey, I was particularly impressed with the bigness of God. I had hit a tee shot that went to the right and landed right in the center of a cluster of trees. As I looked at the ball, not only could I not figure out how it got in there, but how was I going to get it out! Then I remembered the awesomeness of God and I said to Him, "God, if you can do all things, then you can play golf. I am going to hit this and see where you take it."

God took mercy in the infancy of my faith. I took out a club, lined it up to the green with several trees in its path, and hit it. To this day I have no idea how it got out without hitting something, or how it landed on the green. The spectators cheered and I was amazed again at the sovereignty of our Lord. The ball was only about 10 feet from the cup. "Great shot, Lord. You truly can do all things. I'll take it from here!" After all, it was only 10 feet away. Not only can God do amazing things on a golf course, but He also has a way of teaching us life lessons.

It was my turn to learn. All I had to do was to putt the ball into the hole in two strokes. No problem! The first putt went by the hole and stopped about 15 feet beyond it. I could not believe it. I took my time and lined the next putt up and hit it to the hole. It not only didn't go in, but it ended up where I first began. Needless to say, the crowd was very quiet as I lost the hole, but learned the lesson.

Romans 12:1-2 Do not conform any longer to the pattern of this world, but be transformed by the renewing of your mind. Then you will be able to test and approve what God's will is — his good, pleasing and perfect will.

One of the most-asked questions is: "What is God's will for my life?" Most everyone is anxious to know God's will, as if it were some highly complicated secret formula. Usually, we tend to think of doing God's will in terms of doing stuff for God that we really don't feel like doing, and then going back to doing our own thing once the task is complete. It just doesn't work like that. Very simply, as you will see by the following Scriptures, living out God's will means that He wants us to have an incredible ongoing relationship with Him. That means that we will walk with Him no matter where, we will be completely honest with Him no matter what, and that we will be more than willing to take a risk and go outside our comfort zone to do what He asks us to do. It also means that He will be our guide, our purpose for living, our friend and our inspiration. Actually, He becomes our everything. Period.

This much I know about God, He is not into creating lists for us to check off, nor does He want us to take the lead in the relationship we have with Him. Why does He want to have such a relationship with us? Because He loves us; He "blessed us in the heavenly realms with every spiritual blessing in Christ" (Ephesians 1) and that includes giving us life! "I have come that they may have life, and have it to the full" (John 10:10).

God loves you and wants for you to find what you are looking for in life: love, purpose, promise, hope, joy and peace can only be found in Him. He wants you to have all that and more! That is His will for you. How do I walk with God in a meaningful relationship? Scripture speaks for itself.

Matthew 22:37-40 Jesus replied: "Love the Lord your God with all your heart and with all your soul and with all your mind." This is the first and greatest commandment. And the second is like it: "Love your neighbor as yourself." All the Law and the Prophets hang on these two commandments.

1 Peter 2:15-17 For it is God's will that by doing good you should silence the ignorant talk of foolish men. Live as free men, but do not use your freedom as a cover-up for evil; live as servants of God. Show proper respect to everyone:

Love the brotherhood of believers, fear God, honor the king.

God has a passion for the Christian to love and help the poor. An example as to just how much God loves those who serve the poor is found in Matthew 25:34-36 "Then the King will say to those on his right, 'Come, you who are blessed by my Father; take your inheritance, the kingdom prepared for you since the creation of the world. For I was hungry and you gave me something to eat, I was thirsty and you gave me something to drink, I was a stranger and you invited me in, I needed clothes and you clothed me, I was sick and you looked after me, I was in prison and you came to visit me.'

No matter what our jobs may be, we are all called to care for the poor. Andrew, however, tells his story of how God called him into full-time service with children who are in desperate need.

> **Andrew's Story.** Let me start by stating clearly that you do not need to dedicate your life to the poor, the needy and the helpless to do God's work. God has given us all individual gifts that can and should be used in a variety of walks of life—to serve His will, not ours. We should not pursue seminary or any social justice career out of our own motivations to gain any kind of status with God. We should listen intently for His will for our lives. It may well be that God's plan for us is to be available to witness to the fast food customer, the hardware store salesman, or to impact Wall Street in a positive way. That being said, I believe that God has called me, at this point in my life, to work to help abused and neglected children.
>
> The wonderful thing about God's will for your life is how unmistakably clear it can be. I remember going to law school and having no idea what to do when I got out. I will say that, through prayer and study, I was at a point in my life where I felt very close to God. That gave me a sense of peace—a comfort that no matter where I ended up, it would be where He wanted me to be.
>
> My brother, Scott, had moved to Denver and invited me to join him there.
>
> I took him up on his invitation and crashed at his house. There, as I began studying for the bar exam, I was convinced that I wanted to work with children. I had made a promise to myself and to God that I would not let being an attorney corrupt me; I would always strive to make a difference in the world in a positive way, using whatever resources God would give me. After passing the bar exams, I immediately started sending out

resumes to everyone involved in children's law. I was convinced that God's plan was my plan, and it would unfold in front of my eyes. Then I got my first rejection letter, then another, and another. I began to doubt, but remained hopeful. I got a few more rejections, and had some great near misses, and then I began to get frustrated and scared. My sense of calm and peace was waning.

In hopes of getting close again to God, I made a conscious choice to go back to the beginning—to that place where I had felt so close to Him, that I did not worry. I began to spend more daily time with God and prayed for the peace and trust I once knew so well. And a funny thing happened. It worked. God had once again proved Himself to be faithful. I still had no idea what I was to do. I still got rejection letters on a regular basis, but I was not alone; I consciously opened myself up to whatever God had in store for me. With that, I took a job that required me to commute an extra hour to work, at a small firm that had little to nothing to do with child law. It was a hard job that required me to grow both as a man and as an attorney at a very rapid pace. I was placed in many compromising situations where I was forced to make tough decisions under extreme pressure. I was very successful, but I kept thinking there has to be more to God's plan for me. Eventually, I had to make a choice whether to stay or take a leap of faith. I leapt by quitting my job and attempting to go into business for myself.

Another very difficult road. After a few months I had started to grow a small client base, when I got my big break. A client whom I had helped on a small traffic case came into my office (I should say apartment/office) with the million dollar case all young attorneys dream about. Then, about a week later, I got another call. This was from a reputable non-for-profit firm with whom I had interviewed months before (one of the near misses), that offered a position as a child advocate attorney. They wanted to know if I still had a desire to work with them. It was as if God said, "OK—remember all that talking you did about wanting to serve children—remember all those prayers asking for an opportunity to make a difference. Here you go, here's your chance. Just one catch—you have to let go of that million dollar case." Another choice. Do I rely on myself, or do I rely on God? Do I create my own success, or do I find success in the will of my Father? Do I take the job, or not?

I took it. Not because it was the right step for my own personal gain, but because it was His plan at this time for my life. It all became extremely clear again—everything that I had gone through had shaped me into being the right person for this job that God had directed me to take. The tough, uncompromising cases I had survived taught me what I needed to know to be an effective children's attorney, to actually make a difference. Something became clear to me that I will never forget. It is simply this: God is trying constantly to offer His help and guidance to all of us, and all we need to do is release ourselves to what He wants for us, to accept His will for our lives, and He will give us all more than we need.

Making the choice to pursue a job primarily dedicated to helping those who could not help themselves has been more fulfilling than I imagined. I hear horrible stories of children being abused and neglected every day. I visit children in hospitals, foster homes and rehabilitation centers on a regular basis. I am able to stand in the midst of complete chaos and maintain my composure, because I am not alone. God is faithful and is my constant companion. To watch the amazing work of God, as He works through me and into the lives of others, is a profound joy that outweighs any amount of struggle. It is my privilege to be able to serve God in this way.

For those who are gifted in sports, you also have incredible opportunities to be used mightily by God! Not only is Alex a great athlete, but he is a warrior for Christ who does not know what it means to retreat!

Alex's Story. My university, a large ACC school, is one of the best schools in the South. It is very technical and with lots of pretty smart students. It was tough going down there. I remember Nancy, in Anchorsaway, giving an example of a guy in a fraternity who shows up and preaches the Gospel and shares the love of Jesus Christ with his fraternity brothers, but never seems to be getting anywhere. I felt the same way going to my university. It can get very discouraging for a Christian who is trying to make a difference.

I spent four years on the swim team in Division I athletics and labored and labored for Jesus Christ on my team. The first year, I felt like I got nowhere. I preached by living and speaking and holding Bible studies. I got involved with a great campus ministry, but I felt like I didn't get anywhere with my teammates. I really began to question what I was doing at this school and why God had me there. I came back my second year and was even more zealous and on fire for God; preaching the Gospel and serving my teammates. Finally, I began to see some fruit, but like the seed that fell among the thorns, I saw people with faith that sprang up fast, and then was choked and withered. A Scripture that was helpful to me in this time was Philippians 3:12. "Not that I have already obtained this or am already perfect, but I press on to make it my own, because Christ Jesus has made me his own." So I pressed on.

After two years of prayer, God brought me a couple of young Christian guys who were freshmen on the swim team. I was able to challenge them and encourage them in Christ. I have had the privilege of developing a discipleship relationship with them and helping them grow in their faith. Entering my fourth year, God brought me two more freshmen, in whose hearts God was really at work. I have also had the privilege of meeting with them regularly this past year. We would talk about our walks with God and study the Bible together. I am now finished with collegiate swimming, but I know that my time was not wasted. Even though I did not always get my best times, and my swimming career did not end as well as I would have liked, I can see my purpose at college was much greater than how well I swam. I pressed on to live out the Salvation that God has given me. He brought me to this particular place in order for me to be involved in changing the lives of the men on my swim team, and I know I have accomplished that.

Sometimes God moves us into areas where we feel alone and unfamiliar with our surroundings. Responding to a call of God to leave the country not only moved Katie closer to God, but taught her many life lessons that impacted her life now and forever.

Katie's Story. I was getting ready to graduate from college, and I had been praying about what God wanted me to do next. Africa had been on my mind for a couple years ... and as I kept praying Isaiah 6:8 "Here am I, send me," He had me wait.

I visited Uganda, in East Africa, in 2002. It was a great experience and one which I will never forget. We visited villages daily, hosting Bible studies, leading worship and generally encouraging fellow believers. I was there for 12 days. I visited a village where they had never seen white people before. I ate food I was not accustomed to eating and the word "comfort" took on a whole new meaning. My comfort became my traveling companion and Jesus.

I never thought I would go to Africa again, but thankfully, God always has the "bigger picture" in mind for us; a plan that will prosper and not harm. And so, with a growing desire to return to this beloved continent, God opened the doors for me to visit Nairobi, Kenya. On March 4, 2006, I flew to Nairobi, Kenya, which would soon become a place of humility, growth, experience and love.

Immediately when I arrived, my clothing gave me away to be western; instantly giving me a feeling of being an outsider and caused me to ask the question, "What am I doing here?" In the first week, as I learned the streets of Nairobi, and how to accomplish the essentials (grocery shopping, cyber cafes, Mo's house), I quickly became accustomed to the walking. Walking became an important time in my life in Kenya, because it became my barometer for how my day would go. Being an American Caucasian woman gave way to assumptions, stares, and often "cat calls."

Oh, the office … My first day at the office, I was offered tea and was introduced to everyone. This could have easily been one of the most intimidating feelings I had during my stay in Africa. There was a group of about 10 people talking in three different languages. I was convinced that they were talking about me. I just kept thinking, "What am I, a white girl from America, doing over here in Nairobi?" God knew that answer, and within weeks, walls broke down, language became a non-issue and hearts began to open. Soon I was no longer walking in an office of Africans speaking many languages, but I was walking into a family of brothers and sisters … Muhia, Benson, Sammy, Linda, Mwas, Timo, Ken, Janet, Rhoda and Steve.

The feeling of being intimidated had vanished. It was no longer all about me. I knew I could learn so much more and gain from the relationships God had placed in my lap. I learned about culture, not just Kenyan culture, but specifics about different tribes, religions and history. I learned that I can have just as much, if not more, in common with an African, as I can with my next door neighbor in the U.S. I learned that God stretches beyond the oceans. I saw a big picture of God's desire for His kingdom. People from all tribes and tongues singing to the same God! I think I caught a glimpse of heaven!

One of the best, and most humbling, experiences was on my last day at the office. I had gone in for the "send off." We knelt down in a circle, held hands and prayed. Each person said what I meant to them and/or taught them while I was there. They continued to tell me how relational I was, and how well they felt like I knew them and they knew me. Through this, God showed me that I was there for a reason. He took my fear, anxiety and assumptions about a culture that was different than the one that I grew up in, and turned it into the most beautiful experience of my life.

Meet a former student of mine named Phillip, who went to a small private college. He had asked me to pray about his future roommate and I did. Needless to say, I was surprised to receive an email from Phillip telling me that his roommate was a bit different than expected.

Phillip's Story. When I first moved into my new dorm room, I immediately saw a different worldview in my roommate than the one I embrace. He was gay and a Wiccan (witchcraft). Both of these challenged me in ways I never thought possible. My roommate had an altar on his bed to the sun-god Ra, with a cleansing bowl to do rituals. He also had a gay porn screen saver on his computer. At first, I was wondering why God had put me in this situation and what He wanted from me. My parents and I prayed and called my friends and family to pray for me and the decision we should make. That is whether or not I should stay in the room with my roommate, or move out and get another roommate.

:: Follow-up emails

This is Phillip. I'm doing well. I got moved out the day after I sent the chain email out to people. God works wonders, let me tell you. So far everything is going pretty well. I'm in a new room, but I don't have a roommate yet, we are still working on that. But anyway, everything is going great, other than a lot of homework in all my classes.

Phillip again. I'm emailing you back with an update. Yep, I have a roommate who is a really great guy. We requested each other as roommates. I've even gotten him to go to Bible studies with me. I haven't been able to contact my old roommate. Every time I tried to talk to him, he was either not there or would avoid me, so I've kind of decided to back off. If I were to say something to him now, I feel that it would be like pouring lemon in a paper cut.

Phillip's attitude about his roommate amazed me. Here is a guy who understands what it means to walk with God. He was willing to put himself in harm's way on many levels by staying. God released him from this situation.

Maybe God was just testing Phillip; if so, he passed with flying colors. Putting others first and loving the unlovable pleases God.

No matter who you are, or what you do, or where you are in your life, God loves you and wants to give you a life that will fulfill you and glorify Him. It won't always be easy, but it will, no doubt, be the most exhilarating and meaningful journey that you could ever imagine.

I want to close this chapter and really, this book, with a story about a 10-year-old boy named Jared, who lived in Denver. He passed away after battling relapses of leukemia and complications of chemotherapy and bone marrow transplant. We can all talk the talk, but to actually live it out to the death, as Jared did, is another story, altogether. Jesus loved children and wanted them to come to Him. Jared is one who came to Him fully clothed in righteousness. He had a big faith that most of us could only dream about.

Blessings to you as you read Jared's story, may it bless you and encourage you as you continue your journey in discovering the Sovereign God who loves you.

Jared's story. At the memorial service celebrating his life, his uncle spoke of his nephew. Here are a few excerpts from his talk:

"He was only 10, but he lived BIG—with a BIG voice, in a BIG world, and with a BIG faith.

"This past week he has slept with two swords on his bed—a wooden one and a Star Wars light saber—he explained that he was going to be fighting in God's army soon, and wasn't sure which one he would need.

"The last few nights of his life, his parents found him kneeling beside his bed, praying for his family.

"When I asked him what he will do as soon as he sees Jesus, he responded, 'Probably be speechless … then I'll just run to Him!'"

Oh God, give us all a faith like Jared! Amen. :: :: ::

:: **What God?**

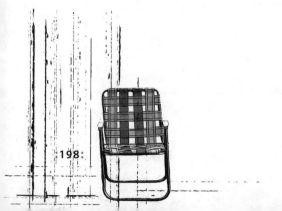

THE LAKE AGAIN ::

conclusion

it is 6:30 a.m. and I am sitting on our dock up in Michigan trying to figure out what just happened. It's July and our kids were home to celebrate the fourth with us at the lake. We had a great time playing croquet, swimming, boating and just hanging out. It was one of those perfect weeks, even the weather cooperated!

The last day of their stay, my husband, Ed, decided to take a ride on a wave runner, our son, Scott, was riding on another one, the tanners were busy soaking up the sun while the kids were swimming. My son, Mark, and I were sailing in a brisk wind and were thoroughly enjoying ourselves. Suddenly, another large wave runner came alongside of our sail boat and yelled, "Mark, come quick, there has been a horrible accident. It's your dad! He was hit by another wave runner." Mark jumped up and looked at me. "Go," I said, "I will be fine. Go!" With that he jumped off the sail boat to the waiting ride that was going to take him to his father.

I went numb, my thoughts were whirling as I scrambled to turn the boat around and head for the island. "Lord God, what is happening?" I felt completely helpless. My husband was in dire straights and I could not be there with him. All I could do was to pray and pray I did. I asked God to show His face to Ed and to bring to him all and more then he needed. I prayed for protection for the kids as they were no doubt living out a nightmare. I prayed for myself that He would give me supernatural strength and faith to deal with whatever was waiting for me.

In the midst of the flurry of prayers, I paused and realized that the wind had died down to a breeze that was filling my sails, and was gently taking me not only to the island, but directly to the buoy. I have sailed for many years, but I had never experienced the obvious presence of God as I did in that moment. If He could calm the wind and carry me to the exact point that I needed to go, then He could take me through whatever lay ahead.

Within minutes I could see the shore and then the dock. There were people in our yard, with some on the dock hovering around a body that was very still.

I had no idea if Ed was alive or in heaven. Immediately I had a flash back of what had happened with Stephen so many years earlier. "Lord, I feel like I have gone full circle … a déjà vu experience. This time, however, I thank You that I know You and for being here with all of us. No matter what, I want this to glorify You. Give me eyes to see the blessings and lessons that You have for me. Thank You that You are here even in the midst of this horrific accident."

The boat glided to the buoy and I jumped off the boat and ran to Ed. He was alive and in good hands. Soon he was loaded into a float boat and escorted by two sheriffs to the waiting ambulance at the island landing. Within minutes he was being cared for at a hospital in Kalamazoo, and soon operated on by a very competent surgeon. Ed had turned his boat into our son by mistake and had broken several ribs, punctured his lungs, broken his femur and shattered his kneecap. All this would heal over time. In the mean time, our home for the next several weeks would be the trauma intensive care unit.

It is now two days after the accident; here I sit, all the kids are gone back to their homes. The sun is coming up and the lake is a glassy calm. I am thinking back on my conversation with God when Stephen died, recalling the fear mixed with a need to know who this God is that would allow such a thing to happen, resulting in my choice to stay away from Him. Now, with another terrible incident, I am looking at the circumstances with new eyes. "God, thank You for making Yourself so evident in the midst of all of this." There were no coincidences. Not only the wind in my sail, the sheriffs who "just happened" to be near the island at the time of the accident who came to our aid immediately; the retired rescue worker who was walking around the island and "just happened" to be in front of our cottage at the time of the accident; the anesthesiologist who was excellent and lived on the island and "just happened" to not only be on-call but in the hospital; as well as the most noted knee surgeon in southwest Michigan who was also on-call and in the hospital. My son, Scott, who escaped injury as their boats collided, is a great swimmer and was able to keep Ed from drowning and swam him to shore. My son, Mark, who is an orthopedic sports medicine surgeon from Denver and who had not been to the lake in four years, was there to help save him and spend the night at the hospital, making sure that all was going well.

"Father, You are so far ahead of me and I pray that You will remind me to continue walking, now and in the days and years to come, behind You. For all you have done and for all You are, I give you great thanks. Amen."

:: **Weeks later**
We have an amazing God who loves us, who communicates with us and desires us not only to know Him, but for us to open the most intimate parts of our lives to His truth, and allow Him to rule us from the inside out. In the midst of our brokenness, failures, loneliness, hurts and doubts, there is God, Our Lord, Who loved us enough to die for us and continues to love us in spite of ourselves, forever! It is one thing for us as humans to love someone, it is quite another to be loved by God who loves us deeper than we would ever imagine, eternally, abundantly and ferociously.

It's been several weeks since that morning on the dock. Ed is recovering slowly. There are going to be many difficult days ahead for us, and I am sure for you, as well, no matter what road you are traveling. Nothing is perfect in this world and suffering is a big part of it.

In light of that, I was thinking of what I could say that would bring to a close the truths that I am trying to communicate in this book. I was reminded of a song that is and has been since it was written in 1860, on the preschool best seller list, "Jesus Loves Me." It was written by Anna Bartlett Warner. I, along with many, think that it is the most simple but profound hymn ever written. It is also where my journey began.

"Jesus loves me this I know, for the Bible tells me so ..." :: :: ::

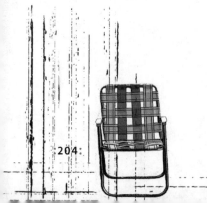

YOUR TURN ::

appendix A

thank you for traveling on this journey with me. My deepest desire is that you will start or continue living a culture-changing life with a Christian worldview as your compass. My hope is that your life will reflect what Christ has done, and is doing in you each and every day. I challenge you to always be ready to share the Truth of Christ and the life that He offers us, to anyone who asks.

If you would like to impact seniors in high school and college students with the Christian worldview, you may want to consider teaching the Anchorsaway curriculum in your community. Many are teaching Anchorsaway to adults in churches and in small group settings as well. It is for anyone who is either questioning their faith or wants to deepen their faith with solid answers from history, science, the Bible and scholars who are experts in their field of expertise. Not only will students of the curriculum learn with clarity about the hope they have, but they will also be armed to answer for their faith with confidence in an unbelieving world!

The curriculum covers 21 major questions that are listed in the following appendix. The Anchorsaway curriculum has been approved for three hours of college credit. Please go to the Anchorsaway website to learn more about this!

For more information about starting an Anchorsaway site in your area, please visit our website at **www.anchorsawayministries.org**

:: **Chapters offered in the Anchorsaway Curriculum:**
1. What is the Christian Worldview?
2. What are the Five Major Worldviews?
3. Who is God?
4. Is the Bible Reliable?
5. Was Jesus Christ Resurrected? Why Does it Matter?
6. Is Jesus Christ God? What is the Trinity?
7. What is a Christian? Am I One?
8. Did Life Just Happen or Were We Created?
9. Who is the god of Islam?
10. What is the Big Picture of God's Redemption of Man?
11. Who is Satan and How Does He Work?
12. What is a Cult?
13. Why Don't the Jews Believe in Jesus?
14. How Does God View the Homosexual?
15. What are the Moral Implications of Bioethics?
16. What is the Christian Role in Cultural Reconciliation?
17. What are the Biblical Principles to Wise Financial Planning?
18. How can I Become a Leader Who Influences Culture for Christ?
19. Why Does God Allow Suffering?
20. How Do I Make Good Life Choices?
21. What are the Keys to Building Healthy Relationships?

:: **What God?**

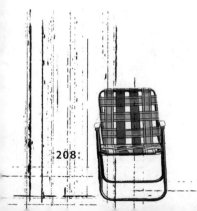

KNOWING FOR SURE ::

appendix B

how do I know for sure?

:: How can I have a personal relationship with God?

If you are sure that you believe that Jesus is God and that you want to have a relationship with God that will not only fulfill your desire to have the peace and joy that is lacking in your life as well as having the assurance that you will live forever with God, then below is a suggested progression. Know that it is not your words but the condition and sincerity of your heart that God looks on. God wants to have a relationship with you much more than you do with Him. He loves you just that much!

1. KNOW that the Holy and loving God of the Bible wants to have a relationship with you, right now, just as you are!

> **John 3:16-19** For God so loved the world that he gave his one and only Son, that whoever believes in him shall not perish but have eternal life. For God did not send his Son into the world to condemn the world, but to save the world through him. Whoever believes in him is not condemned, but whoever does not believe stands condemned already because he has not believed in the name of God's one and only Son.

2. REALIZE that you are a sinner who cannot in any way earn your salvation. Know that you can never do enough good works to merit or deserve a personal relationship with God. It does not matter how "good" you think you have been, or what church you have joined, or with what wonderful philanthropic organizations you have worked, you still are not good enough.

> **Romans 3:21-25** But now a righteousness from God, apart from law, has been made known, to which the Law and the Prophets testify. This righteousness from God comes through faith in Jesus Christ to all who believe. There is no difference, for all have sinned and fall short of the glory of God, and are justified freely by his grace through the redemption that came by Christ Jesus.

> **Romans 6:22-23** For the wages of sin is death, but the gift of God is eternal life in Christ Jesus our Lord.

3. YOU MUST BELIEVE that Jesus Christ is the only way to God. He died for your sins and rose again on the third day for your redemption!

> **1 Corinthians 15:1-5** Now, brothers, I want to remind you of the Gospel

I preached to you, which you received and on which you have taken your stand. By this Gospel you are saved, if you hold firmly to the word I preached to you. Otherwise, you have believed in vain. For what I received I passed on to you as of first importance: that Christ died for our sins according to the Scriptures, that he was buried, that he was raised on the third day according to the Scriptures, and that he appeared to Peter, and then to the Twelve.

It is not good works plus Christ, Buddha plus Christ, nor your church membership plus Christ. It is faith in Jesus alone.

John 14:6 (Jesus speaking) "I am the way, the truth and the life; no man cometh unto the father but by me."

4. COME to Jesus in faith, believing the Gospel, and ask Him to be your Savior. You can talk to Him like you can talk to a living person, because He does live and is ever present wherever you are. He said, Himself: John 6:37-38 "All that the Father gives me will come to me, and whoever comes to me I will never drive away."

5. ONCE YOU ARE SAVED you can go to a good Bible teaching church. You will start to grow from a "baby" Christian to a mature Christian, always remembering that you are His forever!

1 John 5:13 I write these things to you who believe in the name of the Son of God so that you may know that you have eternal life.

If you have made such a commitment, let me welcome you into the family of God! Be sure to tell the friend that gave you this book or someone that would celebrate with you and encourage you on your new journey with Christ. :: :: ::

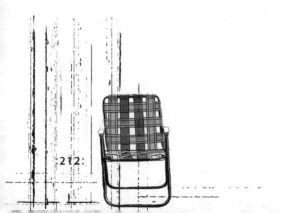

SMALL GROUP DISCUSSION GUIDE ::

appendix C

:: **What God?**

Questions for further discussion

:: introduction **THE LAKE**

1. What is your greatest accomplishment in life? Who or what has told you this was a "great" accomplishment?
2. What do you do for a living and why do you do it?
3. What is your purpose for living?
4. Are you living in a way that is fulfilling your purpose?
5. Using short answers, discuss as a group the answers to the following questions.
   - From where did I come?
   - Why is there such a mess in the world?
   - What hope do I have?
   - What happens when I die?
   - What is my purpose in life?

:: chapter 1 **PREACHERS**

1. Discuss this quote: "Being a Christian is like being a lady. If you have to tell someone that you are, most likely you're not."
2. Read these questions aloud to your group and have people reflect on them silently. How do your answers reflect your worldview?
   - What do you spend most of your time doing?
   - Where do you spend your money?
   - When people ask you about your life, what do you tell them?
   - What do you value the most in life?
3. Based on the different worldviews that you encountered in this chapter, which one does your life reflect the most? Are there areas in your life that are representative of a worldview other than the Christian worldview?
4. What is your life "preaching" to your friends, family and the world?
5. If you were never allowed to speak, would your life mirror Christ's love and Truth? In what ways would this be possible?

:: chapter 2 **the book or THE BOOK**

1. Do you have a life motto? What is it and why is this motto important to you?
2. What do you think is the world's biggest hesitation about the Bible? What do you think is the reason for this hesitation?
3. Does it take more faith to believe the Bible or to NOT believe it is Truth and inspired by God?
4. How does your life change knowing Scripture is the inerrant Word of God?
5. What keeps you from being a student of the Bible?

:: chapter 3 **ROAD BLOCKS**

1. Do you have specific road blocks when it comes to your faith? What are they?
2. Can road blocks be good?
3. In this chapter you read about three different types of doubt, Stubborn Doubt, Reasonable Doubt and Heartfelt Doubt. Which one of these do you struggle with in your own life?
4. Is it possible to doubt God, while trusting Him?
5. What will it take for the road blocks in your life to be eliminated?

:: chapter 4 **DEAD OR ALIVE**

1. Discuss the following: Jesus, a good man versus Jesus, conqueror of death?
2. Do you live out an attitude of hope? In what or in whom is it anchored?
3. Explain the magnitude of Christ's death on the cross.
4. What difference does it make to you personally that Jesus died for your sins?
5. Is it possible to have hope and not believe in the resurrection of Jesus Christ?

:: chapter 5 **TOOLS OF THE TRADE**

1. Review the 5 "L"s :
   Learn the foundations of the Christian Faith
   Live out their faith in all of life
   Listen to others
   Love unconditionally
   Lead others to an authentic faith in Jesus Christ
2. To whom do you go for advice about life? Why do you allow them to speak into your life?
3. In this chapter you learned the 5 "L"s. Is this a model similar to the one you apply personally when building relationships with others? Why or why not?
4. In regard to the 5 "L"s, which do you practice the least?
5. Did Jesus follow the 5 "L"s?

:: chapter 6 **IT'S ALL IN THE NAME**

1. Describe the being of God.
2. What does the existence of the Trinity reveal to you about God's character?
   • What person of the Trinity do you understand the least?
   • What person of the Trinity do all cults and false religions misrepresent?
   • What difference does it make if you believe in Jesus as long as you believe in God?

:: chapter 7 **AM I?**
1. If you saw Jesus on the streets today, what would He be doing?
2. What makes someone an authentic Christian?
3. In your opinion are most people who claim to be Christians today authentic Christians or Neo-Christians?
4. What turns people away from Christianity?
5. If everyone in your community lived as you did, would there be a revolution for God's kingdom in your area?

:: chapter 8 **IN THE BEGINNING**
1. How do you explain the creation of the world?
2. Why is the creation vs. evolution debate so prominent in our society?
3. Discuss this statement: "The way we view the creation of the world will determine every facet of our living."
4. Do you think it is fair to say that the majority of the world has been deceived by "scientific" findings regarding the history and creation of the world?
5. What are some questions that you might ask an evolutionist?

:: chapter 9 **CLASSROOM COMBAT**
1. Discuss this quote: "People who live defensively never rise above being average." Are you living out your faith defensively or offensively?
2. Why are many Christians hesitant to stand up for Christianity?
3. Why is it that so many Christians are thought of as "intellectually challenged" when it comes to discussing what they believe to be true?
4. Do you think that it is more important to win a debate or to cause a person to consider an outside opinion?
5. What speaks louder to the world, walking your faith or talking your faith?

:: chapter 10 **DEADLY QUESTIONS**
1. Are you on the path leading toward something absolutely marvelous, or something absolutely mediocre?
2. Does the path that leads towards a life that is "absolutely marvelous" have anything to do with your ability to be an active participant in conversation that calls attention to the truth of Scripture?
3. Have you been misled by untruths because you didn't ask the right questions?
   • Do you think that most people who believe ideas that are contrary to the Bible have done their research to support those ideas?
   • If you have used this line of questioning, how far did you get?

:: chapter 11 **SATAN'S GAMES**
1. Does the devil know who you are?
2. Are you living your life in a way that would get Satan's attention?
3. In what ways do you see Satan working in the world today?
4. Satan tempts us, God tests us. What is the difference?
5. What is the difference between coexisting with darkness versus opposing darkness?

:: chapter 12 **HOW COULD GOD?**
1. Where do we get the idea that suffering is not a part of this life?
2. Why is there suffering in this world?
3. Is the end result of suffering always bad?
4. How does the presence of suffering affect your relationship with Jesus Christ?
5. Would you be more or less effective in comforting others who struggle with pain and suffering if you had not suffered yourself?

:: chapter 13 **OH, SO THAT'S WHO YOU ARE!**
1. What is your response to the common belief that "All religions worship the same god, just in different ways?"
2. What sets our God apart from all other gods?
3. What attribute of God amazes you?
4. How have you seen God work lately?
5. In spite of the mess in this world, how do you know that God really loves and cares for you?

:: chapter 14 **LIVE IT!**
1. What one thing should you eliminate from your life that holds you back from living out the Christian worldview?
2. How can you show others you are a lover of Christ in environments that may frown upon open talk of religion and faith?
3. What does the Holy Spirit have to do with living out the Christian worldview?
4. What qualifies someone as being poor? What are you doing to meet the needs of the poor that God has brought into your life?
5. What do you want your life to say to others?

RESOURCES ::

end notes

:: What God?

:: chapter 1 **PREACHERS**

1 Jill Carattini, Ravi Zacharias International Ministries, [Slice 1451] Matters of the Heart (June 29, 2007).

:: chapter 2 **the book or THE BOOK**

1 Josh McDowell, Evidence that Demands a Verdict (Here's Life Publishers, Inc, 1979).

2 The information in this section was adapted from page 14 of "Discovering the Bible: A simple introduction to the Bible, what it is, how we got it, and how to use it," the publication accompanying the video series, Discovering the Bible, prod. Gateway Films, Worchester, PA. video series. Christian History Institute, 1996.

3 Floyd McElveen, God's Word, Final, Infallible and Forever (Grand Rapids: Gospel Truth Ministries, 1985) 19.

4 Peter Stoner, Science Speaks (Chicago: Moody Press, 1958), ed. Donald W. Stoner, 2002, 29 March 2005, chap. 3.

5 Ibid.

6 This page came from Bryant C. Wood, "In what ways have the discoveries of archeology verified the reliability of the Bible?", 1995, Associates of Biblical Research, 30 March 2005 <http://www.christiananswers.net/q-abr/abr-a008.html>.

7 Eusebius, Ecclesiastical History III.39 found in McDowell, Evidence That Demands a Verdict, 63.

8 Flavius Josephus, The Works of Josephus, trans. William Whiston (Peabody, MA: Hendrickson Publishers, Inc., 1987) 480.

:: chapter 3 **ROAD BLOCKS**

1 Vine's Expository Dictionary of Biblical Words, Copyright © 1985, Thomas Nelson Publishers.

2 Biblesoft's New Exhaustive Strong's Numbers and Concordance with Expanded Greek-Hebrew Dictionary. Copyright © 1994, 2003 Biblesoft, Inc. and International Bible Translators, Inc.

3 The Wycliffe Bible Commentary, Electronic Database. Copyright © 1962 by Moody Press.

:: chapter 4 **DEAD OR ALIVE**

1 W. E. Vine, An Expository Dictionary, 616.

2 Josh McDowell, Evidence That Demands a Verdict, vol. 1 (1979; Nashville: Thomas Nelson Publishers, 1999) 190-191.

:: chapter 6 IT'S ALL IN THE NAME

1   Richard Wightman Fox, Jesus In America (San Francisco: HarperCollins, 2004) 5.
2   C. S. Lewis, Mere Christianity (1952; San Francisco: HarperCollins, 2001) 51-52.

::chapter 7 AM I?

1   George Barna, The Second Coming of the Church (Nashville: Word Publishing Group, 1998) 25.
2   The Barna Update "A Biblical Worldview Has a Radical Effect on a Person's Life," 1 December 2003.
3   Vine's Expository Dictionary of New Testament Words.
4   Happy Christmas! And Happy Easter! —Cindy Hess Kasper.
5   Adapted from David Roper, "A Fresh and Better Start," sermon, 20 June 1996, Idaho Mountain Ministries, 6 April 2005 <http://www.pbc.org/dp/dcroper/models/0004freshstart.html>.
6   This page came from Neil Anderson, Victory Over the Darkness, 2nd ed. (Ventura, CA: Regal Books, 2000) 51-53.
7   Ibid.

::chapter 8 IN THE BEGINNING

1   Chuck Colson, Answers to Your Kids' Questions (Wheaton, IL: Tyndale House Publishers, Inc., 2000) 38.
2   Denton, Evolution: Theory in Crisis, 261-262.
3   Kyle Butt, "Biogenesis – The Long Arm of the Law," ApologeticsPress.org 2002, Apologetics Press 13 April 2005 <http://www.apologeticspress.org/modules.php?name=Read&itemid=1769&cat=3>.
4   George Wald, "The Origin of Life," The Scientific American Aug. 1954: 45-46.
5   Michael Rose, "Slap and Tickle in the Primeval Soup," New Scientist, vol. 112 Oct. 30, 1986: 55.
6   Kathleen McAuliffe, "Why We have Sex," Omni Dec. 1983: 18. Quoted in Walt Brown, In the Beginning, 65.
7   Michael J. Behe, "Darwin's Hostages: A decision in Kansas to question evolution dogma has given rise to hysteria and intolerance," The American Spectator Dec. 1999 - Jan. 2000: Access Research Network 19 April 2005 <http://www.arn.org/docs/behe/mb_darwinshostages.htm>.

:: chapter 9 **CLASSROOM COMBAT**
1   BreakPoint Worldview, March 2007 page 15.

:: chapter 10 **DEADLY QUESTIONS**
1   Thanks to Andrew Heister, Jeff Myers, & Mark Cahill for the four deadly
questions which have been used for many years in the teaching at
Summit Ministries (Colorado Springs, CO). As a frequent educator at
Summit, Mark Cahill effectively explains these penetrating questions in
this book. Mark Cahill, One Thing You Can't Do In Heaven (Bartlesville,
OK: Genesis Publishing Group, 2004) 139-146.

:: chapter 11 **SATAN'S GAMES**
1   Dave Hunt, Occult Invasion (Harvest House, 1998).
2   Jerald and Sandra Tanner, 3,913 Changes in the Book of Mormon (Salt
Lake City: Utah Lighthouse Ministry, 1996). Also see
<http://www.utlm.org/onlinebooks/3913intro.htm>.
3   Jerald & Sandra Tanner, Mormonism-Shadow or Reality? (Salt Lake City:
Utah Lighthouse Ministry, 1987, Fifth Edition) 474-483.
4   Joseph Smith, Journal of Discourses, Volume 6, (1844) 3-5. Also see:
Bob Witte, Where Does It Say That? (Grand Rapids: Gospel Truths).
5   Joseph Smith, Journal of Discourses, Volume 6, (1844) 8. Also see:
Brigham Young, Journal of Discourses, Volume 8 (1860) 268.
6   Joseph Fielding Smith, Doctrines of Salvation, Volume 1, 39. Also see:
Jerald & Sandra Tanner, Mormonism-Shadow or Reality? (Salt Lake City:
Utah Lighthouse Ministry, 1987, Fifth Edition) 171-172.
7   Wayne Grudem, Systematic Theology: An Introduction to Biblical
Doctrine (Grand Rapids: Zondervan, 1994) 226, 231.
8   Orson Pratt, The Seer (1853) 172.
9   Bruce McConkie, The Mortal Messiah, Volume 4, 434.
10 Orson Pratt, The Seer (1853) 158. Also see: Bob Witte, Where Does It Say
That? (Grand Rapids, Gospel Truths) 4-7.
11 Bruce McConkie, Speech given at BYU devotional (March 2, 1982).
12 Book of Mormon, II Nephi 25:23.
13 Joseph Smith, Journal of Discourses, Volume 6, (1844) 3-4. Also see:
Bob Witte, Where Does It Say That? (Grand Rapids: Gospel Truths).
14 Joseph Smith, History of the Church, Volume 1, 283.
15 Joseph Fielding Smith, Doctrines of Salvation, Volume 2, 133.
16 Joseph Fielding Smith, Doctrines of Salvation, Volume 2, 183. Also see:
Jerald & Sandra Tanner, Mormonism-Shadow or Reality? (Salt Lake City:
Utah Lighthouse Ministry, 1987, Fifth Edition) 198-199.

17 Ibid., 93.

18 The Mormon meanings associated with the previous ten different doctrinal expressions come from Agusta Harting, Families Against Cults of Indiana, 26 April 2005 <http://www.familiesagainstcults.org>.

:: **chapter 12 HOW COULD GOD?**

1 C.S. Lewis, The Problem of Pain, (New York: Macmillan Publishing Co. 1978) 89.

:: **chapter 13 SO THAT'S WHO YOU ARE!**

1 A. W. Tozer, The Knowledge of the Holy (San Francisco: HarperCollins, 1961) 1.

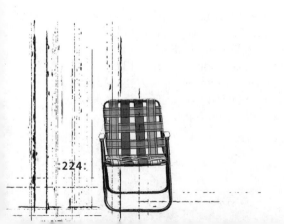